Advance praise for
Sprouting Seeds of Radical Education

It is not often that catalysts and facilitators of change narrate their own journeys of change. This book brings together such narratives from diverse contexts and experiences. It re-affirms the significance of learning for transformational change, every time, every where.

Dr. Rajesh Tandon, Founder-President, PRIA; Dean, PRIA International Academy; UNESCO Co-chair Community-based Research

This book brings back many memories of how reflections on my own journey contributed to my ability to encourage change in Zambia and the world. The richness of sharing those journeys is demonstrated here as is the power of each one of us cross-pollinating each other with insights from the journeys we continue to travel in making a just world.

Dr. Emily Sikazwe, Vice Chair, Zambia Electoral Commission

These essays not only provide us with knowledge, skills and approaches to apply in the field, but through the inspiration and wisdom reflected here, motivate us as a community of practice to keep on with hope, optimism and aspiration.

Saloni Singh, President, Coady Alumni Association of Nepal (CAAN)

This collection of essays demonstrates that seeds of radical education have been planted in diverse parts of the world and are now sprouting. They are what John Lewis would call … 'Make Good Trouble.' Indeed, these stories reflect the various and often challenging roads we must navigate to shift how we think to make transformational change.

Wayn Hamilton, Executive Director, African Nova Scotian Affairs, Government of Nova Scotia

Sprouting Seeds
of Radical Education

Stories of Transformative Change
from Around the World

Editors:
Debbie Castle, David Fletcher, Olga Gladkikh

ISBN: 979-8-88555-969-0 (India)

Published by
People Development, Antigonish, NS, Canada.
www.pdltd.net
and
APMAS, Hyderabad, India
www.apmas.org

Available from www.amazon.in
and local booksellers

Dedication

This book is dedicated to
those who have shared their stories in this collection,
those who wished to contribute and could not at this time,
all friends, families, communities, organizations
and ancestors who support their work,

and

all those who stand for social justice.

Contents

Foreword

Dr. Maureen Coady

I grew up in the ancestral home of Moses Coady at a time when his radical ideas, and those of his cousin Jimmy Tompkins, had captured the imagination of others seeking a more just and equitable world. As Coady's grandniece, I was exposed at an early age to their collective vision of a self-sustaining economic system in eastern Nova Scotia, rooted in community and supported by a citizenry enlightened through adult education. Social emancipatory learning and economic co-operation served as the seeds of the Antigonish Movement that emerged during their work in the Extension Department at St. Francis Xavier University (StFX) in the first half of the 20th century.

As a young girl in 1959 I witnessed the creation of the Coady International Institute, which propelled the Antigonish Movement into an approach that attracted community development practitioners from around the world who also sought to improve socio-economic conditions and promote social justice in their countries. The annual visits of participants to the "Coady homestead" were a privilege for my family to host. Subsequently as a faculty member in the Department of Adult Education at StFX, I have been privileged to work with many Coady participants and with Coady teaching staff. I've witnessed their shared commitment to radical adult education which, in the words of Brazilian educator Paulo Freire (1972), "engages citizens in action and reflection on their world in order to engage in a conscious act, the transformation of reality."[1]

Sprouting Seeds of Radical Education is an important follow up to the very successful Seeds of Radical Education at the Coady Institute: An Anthology of Personal Essays published in 2019. The first anthology provided deep insight into the radical emancipatory model of adult education practiced by the editors and authors of the collection during the past 30 years. The second anthology is a testament to the passion and commitment of these editors and educators. It features essays by Coady graduates and associates who are taking this model of emancipatory learning forward, spreading and sprouting the seeds of radical education around the world.

This anthology moves beyond defining radical adult education to explore the many creative ways its authors are leading deep participatory processes that are motivating social change in diverse communities around the globe. Like Coady and Tompkins, these practitioners are acutely aware of the need for new forms of thinking and action, and are helping citizens to overcome pessimism, unlearn old patterns of thinking, open their minds to new possibilities, and to believe in themselves and their ability to create peace, justice and equity. They are innovating facilitation methods that help people to reimagine their futures and to take actions that can transform their lives, institutions and societies. The authors recognize the power of these practices to create opportunities for those living on the margins to find their voice, tell their stories, and to be heard by others.

Today these global practitioners are continuing the work of Coady, Tompkins, and women such as Zita O'Hearn Cameron and the Sisters of St. Martha who worked alongside them. They are engaging people in their communities to learn together and to take action on critical 21st century issues such as reconciliation, gender equality and climate change. They are contributing to making meaningful systemic and structural changes that will benefit all citizens in their countries. I cannot help but think my Grand Uncle Moses would be very pleased.

Dr. Maureen Coady

Endnote

1 Freire, P. (1972). Pedagogy of the oppressed. New York, NY: Herder and Herder, p. 180.

One

Introduction:
Seeds are sprouting!

Welcome friends to **Sprouting Seeds of Radical Education**. This collection of personal essays shares the stories of 26 individuals from 10 nations around the globe. These individuals have dedicated their lives in various ways to making the world a better, more equitable and just place. Their stories recount the mind shifts, the struggles, the synchronicities, the support of mentors, the special skills and the learning that led to transformative changes in themselves, in others and in their communities. The authors specifically talk about their commitment to lifelong learning and the role that radical education plays in their lives. It is a diverse array of stories connected by the fact that each author, at some point on their journey, linked with the Coady International Institute in the small town of Antigonish, Nova Scotia, Canada.

This book evolved iteratively through 2020 and early 2021, but its seed was planted in 2019 with the publication of Seeds of Radical Education at the Coady Institute[1]. That book, an anthology of personal essays, captured the principled learning approach used at the Coady over the previous 30 years with community development leaders from around the world. The essays touched on philosophy, principles and values; facilitating change processes; and spreading the seeds. Most of them were written by individuals who taught at the Coady over a number of years, graduates who later became co-facilitators, or people involved in running the Institute in various ways. While celebrating that book, many asked about the graduates and their organizations — had the seeds planted in the hallways and classrooms at the Coady taken root and sprouted to make a difference in graduates' communities in other parts of the world? This book was born from those questions, with contributions primarily from graduates.

The voices of 26 change agents are reflected in these pages; 26 stories out of the thousands of people working around the world for change. We reached out to many people who had shared stories about the influence of the Coady on their lives and these are the stories that found their way here. While on the path we have taken to develop this book, not all seeds germinated and grew. Some fell on fertile ground; others faced more hostile environments. It is exciting, however, when seeds do take root, sprout and begin to flourish in a new environment, making a real difference in people's lives. Perhaps the plants have not fully grown, but there is evidence they are healthy and robust and will continue to grow. It is those kind of "sprouting" stories which are shared here.

The pathway to completing this book has been a challenging one as the world was consumed by the COVID-19 pandemic during the time the essays were being written. Luckily, with communication technology, the writers group could have online meetings to support each other, and the editors lived in close enough proximity to meet face-to-face. Writing partners developed for some, bringing people together across diverse contexts because they were working on similar themes. For all, the importance of their work in creating justice and equity in the world through deep participatory engagement was reaffirmed.

With the global reach of the writers group, we were able to connect with what was happening in people's lives, their work and the pandemic. From diverse parts of Canada to India, Nepal, the Caribbean and various countries on the African continent, we got snapshots into the experiences people were having. Those experiences varied and changed over time as the pandemic took its course and the official responses in different countries varied. Most people fared well during this time, but as this book is being finalized the pandemic is entering a new phase. We send our deepest sympathy to one of our authors, Alice Ndlovu, from Zimbabwe who lost her husband, Tinashe Mutanda, to COVID-19 at the end of 2020.

Many of the authors in this collection are first time authors. As development professionals and social justice activists they have written proposals, briefing papers and reports (usually in their native language, not English), but they had not captured and shared a specific story of change in which they played a central role. We are honoured to share their story in this collection.

One aspect of radical education has been captured by feminist Carol Hanisch[2] in the phrase "the personal is political." This collection of personal stories demonstrates how political, economic and social change is driven by individuals' actions and how they live their lives.

In the first book, Seeds of Radical Education, we defined six other aspects of radical education. It is education that:

- nurtures the belief people have within them to create a world of justice, peace and equity for all.
- deviates from conventional approaches to learning and knowledge acquisition by challenging people in the learning process to go deeper in their own reflection and understanding of why they believed what they did.
- embodies care and respect; love is present in the hearts and minds of people learning together.
- practices radical empathy. Effort is put into creating an environment of family, community and support to enable participants to feel safe enough to learn, and to unlearn.
- questions the formal structures of society, entrenched values and practices that have marginalized many and benefited the few.
- seeks radical change in society — changes to create a more just and peaceful world for all. This means inspiring citizen power and building confidence in the voice of active citizens and their capacity to take collective actions. This can seem disruptive for those with power and privilege.

We have grouped the essays in this book into four thematic sections related to change — Leadership, Unlearning, Art and Facilitation.

The first section concerns Leadership for Change. These five personal essays take place in Egypt, Kenya, Nepal, India and Ghana. They address establishing a school between two communities traditionally in conflict, promoting youth leadership, supporting human rights defenders, and standing up for gender justice. All five stories demonstrate the commitment and risk individuals take to work as leaders with others for change. In the first essay, Bashiratu Kamal describes how she became a fearless advocate for gender justice and the rights of all marginalized people. She shares what inspires her — her mother, her schooling opportunities, and the work she continues to do as a spokesperson for the feminist movement in Ghana.

Maina Wambugu Sebastian's story begins as a child growing up in a very poor situation in rural Kenya. He describes how, with the support of his mother and the community he was able to get a degree in agronomy and launch a small NGO. His story does not stop there, however, as Maina dreamed of creating a school for children of agriculturalists and pastoralists in neighbouring communities to transform the recurring conflicts between them.

Ehab Gamal of Egypt writes about establishing youth groups in a slum area in Cairo before the Arab Spring. He describes his journey during the revolution, becoming a human rights defender (HRD), and his need to go into exile. He also discusses the relationship between HRDs and friends outside their own country and offers suggestions for how to support HRDs.

Suran Maharjan starts his story as a 22-year-old, one of the youngest ever in the Coady's Diploma Program. Through his drive and enthusiasm, he goes on to head numerous international youth leadership programs, and continues to challenge himself and motivate other youth to take up leadership opportunities as they emerge.

The final essay is a dialogue between Mary Ramsis of Egypt and Shaiju Chacko of India, two graduates of the 2011 Coady Diploma Program. Mary and Shaiju share the challenges and complexities of integrating their learning into their work and their lives after returning from a transformative learning experience.

The essays in the second section are about the importance of Unlearning to Change. Spanning the globe from the Anishinabek (First Nation in Canada) to Zimbabwe, these six essays all touch on the need to unlearn old patterns and ways of doing and to create new ways of thinking that make space for fresh ideas to emerge. We are invited in these essays to acknowledge the hard work required to break old patterns and challenge ourselves to be humble in our thinking when the pathway to the future seems clear. Obstacles show up to test our new way of thinking and being.

In the first essay, Alice Ndlovu, Zimbabwe, shares her experience of moving from a strict professional organization back to her own community to work with farmers and the clash of cultures inside herself that ensued. She reveals her road to self-discovery including the hard work of doing historical colonial analysis and gaining an appreciation for indigenous knowledges and spirituality.

As a member of the Anishinabek Nation, Corey Wesley articulates how his personal story reflects the catastrophic disruption of Indigenous people and how reclaiming circular systems thinking and an appreciation for interconnectedness can help reconnect with powerful ancestral mental models for cultural revitalization.

Pamela Johnson, Canada, recounts her story of questioning institutional norms for promoting accessibility for people with disabilities. She speaks of the danger of idolizing institutions and people's good intentions when what is really needed is ongoing commitment and persistence in addressing issues to disrupt, dismantle and rebuild institutions to become just and equitable.

Continuing on the institutionalizing theme, Balakrishna Venkatesh, India, reflects on his work experiences with organizations that serve persons with disabilities. He invites us to consider the tensions between allegiances formed within and outside organizations, and accountability to the communities/constituencies the organization has been designed to serve. Using specific examples, he demonstrates the dilemmas that arise and the need to nurture accountability on an ongoing basis.

A deeply personal story of unexpected shifts that can happen in our lives is related by Daren Okafo, Canada. It challenges us to constantly be in a state of becoming. He reminds us never to assume community, but rather to truly hold that ideal in our hearts and minds, to be critical and explicitly define connections and relationships as a key component of the world we wish to generate.

Art for Change makes up the third section of essays. The power of various art forms as processes to take learners deep into their own learning and societies striving for justice is demonstrated in these essays. John Milad Gad brings us his story of working with arts for social change and transformation based on a philosophy that people can discover the power within to heal themselves. From his work supporting people through the violence, pain and fear of the revolution in Egypt to meeting with President Obama, he weaves a story that demonstrates the vital role arts can play in healing for change.

Setting up an arts school as an economic empowerment model for people afflicted by leprosy became a mission for Lazarus Udayakumar, India. He describes how, even today, the exclusion of people with leprosy from society can "extinguish their light," and how painting and selling their art work has the potential to give them the choice to move away from begging and develop their self-esteem.

Graphic dialogue and playful experimentation are mechanisms described by Darren C Brown, Canada, to help groups go deep in transformative learning. He describes how simple visuals can unleash collective creativity, initiate curiosity and reflection, strengthen inclusion and provide collective maps of contexts and systems.

The fourth section of essays focuses on Facilitation for Change. Practitioner-authors from Egypt, Grenada, Canada, Hungary and India share their stories of how particular approaches to facilitation can help engage people in non-judgmental ways, heal through listening, break cultures of silence around bullying, innovate new ways of working with networks, and build authentic peoples' institutions.

The first essay is written by four women from Egypt: Mary Ramsis, Nawal Ghatas, Cynthia Khoury and Victoria Morcos, all graduates of the Coady at different times who previously did not know each other. Their essay tells the story of how they connected in Egypt around the power of facilitation, shared reflections, their desire to promote open and respectful spaces, accept individual talents and creativity, and develop conducive environments oriented to people and relationships.

maureen st. clair writes about the Grenada Listening Project and the fundamental need for listening and radical empathy to work with people to transform conflict situations. Her experiences challenge us to think of compassionate ways to overcome shared histories of human trauma.

A personal story of the trauma of workplace bullying in Canada is conveyed by Susan MacKay as she tells how the experience motivated her to learn and develop training modules for others to prevent and heal from bullying. She concludes with a plea to cultivate communities of kindness and compassion, and to recognize the power of our words to empower or disempower.

In the fourth essay, Darren C Brown and Dániel Törő reflect on their time facilitating online during the COVID-19 crisis and how transformative learning and change can be strengthened with virtual networking and dialogue. They articulate a number of insights and tips for harnessing the magical opportunities that are possible and point out some of the real challenges and bottlenecks along the way.

Three experienced change agents: CS Reddy, Anuj Jain and David Fletcher recount a conversation where they explored how a focus on participation and participatory methods has been effective in building peoples' institutions. Their discussion touches on the evolution of an organization CS founded in India to promote self-help groups, the co-development of certificate courses in Canada, India, Ethiopia and Mexico, and CS's continued commitment to building peoples' institutions through capacity building for his staff.

We are confident you will appreciate learning from these personal accounts of "sprouting seeds of radical education." In addition to a "good read" our wish is that these stories will inspire you to think about your own education, practice and ongoing learning. The essays explore the challenges of being a "good" radical educator with different groups, the importance of building relationships, and understanding what transformative change looks and feels like at the community level. As you read, we ask you to think about:

- What in this story resonates with your own challenges to think differently about conventional ways of doing things?
- How is your experience of "seeding and sprouting" change similar or different to the stories recounted here?
- At this time, what is shifting around you that invites you to consider how the insights shared in these stories might be beneficial to you, your community and your organization?
- What in each anecdote helps you find your own footing to apply some of the principles of radical education?

We invite you to read, reflect and enjoy the personal stories of transformative change that follow.

David, Debbie and Olga

Endnotes

1   Castle, D., Fletcher, D., Gladkikh, O. (2019). Seeds of Radical Education at the Coady Institute: An anthology of personal essays. Antigonish, NS: People Development. www.pdltd.net Available from amazon.com

2 The phrase, "the personal is political" was a rallying cry of second wave feminism in the 1970s. It has been used by many people in social justice movements over the years to challenge people to recognize how they live their own lives is a political act that can either maintain the status quo or lead to changes in society to make it more just and equitable. Feminist Carol Hanisch is credited with the phrase, but she argues its usage grew organically from the work many people were doing to raise political consciousness. For more information see https://www.britannica.com/topic/the-personal-is-political

Leadership for Change

*The world, the way it is,
is not the way it has to be.*

Rev. Dr. Moses Coady
Masters of Their Own Destiny, 1939

Two

Becoming! The path to fighting for a just world

Bashiratu Kamal, Ghana

"We desire above all that men and women will discover and develop their own capacities for creation."

Rev. Dr. Moses Coady[1]

No one knows where their river of life will lead them. I never could have imagined as a girl in Ghana that one day I would be leading national campaigns for women's rights. Growing up in a community and home with few to no professional mentors, I had no one to look up to in the pursuit of education, women's emancipation and career development. My mother was the first point to understanding women's role in society. I was awed by her strength, perseverance, belief in the importance of education despite being illiterate, and her strength in dismantling toxic gendered narratives in raising my brother and me.

I was lucky to have a mother who fought all patriarchal structures and systems to help me have a voice and believe in myself as a human being in a house of over 100 occupants. Brought up in a compound house with tenants of different cultural and religious backgrounds, there was a common belief that women were helpers and secondary to men. My mother refused to allow me to fit into that stereotype. She allowed me to play football with the boys, climb trees and to generally identify as a human being before my gender. This contributed to my ability to never be afraid to pursue my dreams and aspirations.

Inspired by my mom's example, I was determined to be an example to my siblings and to the many girls in my community. She was resilient, empowered and the epitome of an emancipated woman. She didn't have any formal education because, as she said, "School was not my place, business was, and I needed all the respect any man had; I noticed most of it came with having money so I focused on making it too." Her traits influenced my choice of a husband and ability to show everyone that marriage was not a hindrance to aspirations. I completed my first degree with a child and being seven months pregnant. This was possible in part because of the emotional and financial support of my husband who played the dual role of father and mother to the children, supporting my mother in raising our children.

Some of these things I did not appreciate until participating in the River of Life exercise when I was studying at the Coady International Institute in 2017. That exercise presented an opportunity for me to be in a space where my mind and being was peaceful and open to reflecting on my journey. I reflected on the different stages of my life and struggles along the way, acknowledging the many people who have inspired my journey. The rare opportunity to then share my journey with a stranger, who had a different story growing up, made me appreciative of my late mother's role in my life which to this day is leading me to support others in their own emancipatory journey. Through it all, I accepted the challenge to become appreciative of my life, to imagine and see the future I desired, whilst recognizing the power of choice and privilege to overcome the trials I have endured.

Going through self-awareness is difficult, but that deep introspection and the ability to connect it to the world led to some lighter moments with colleagues. However, when I learned that my mother had passed from an auto accident, my resilience was tested. I was only three months into studying at the Coady and I considered going home. How could I spend three months on the other side of the world when I just wanted to grieve this great loss in my life? I realized, however, that being there was divine and I might never get such an opportunity again. The Coady's philosophy to help participants understand themselves and the world in new ways through new knowledge, skills and attitudes was what I needed. I became a humanist facilitator, believing in not knowing it all and always facilitating through stimulation, asking questions and being positive. Learning about the dangers of a single story encouraged me to not be judgmental, whilst becoming conscious of my personality to always create opportunities for others to be seen and heard.

The grief and loneliness from the demise of my mother coupled with my challenging health condition at the Coady led me to be hospitalized for blood transfusions. As a determined soul, I could not end this journey I had set out on.

Finding Resilience
My journey to the Coady started in 2016 when I lost an election that was meant to break me because of my strong personality and my refusal to bend to pressures to go against vulnerable people. After losing the election to become the youth organizer of the national youth council of the Trades Union Congress Ghana, I decided to reposition myself in a way that allowed me to support grassroots union members through policy, programming and legislation. I worked to be part of the journey towards emancipating women within the union movement in Ghana. My commitment to women's rights and social justice is what got me nominated as a student to the Coady by the Network for Women's Right in Ghana (NETRIGHT).

The strength I got from the untold stories of my life during the River of Life exercise was enough to propel me to fulfill this dream for myself, my late mother and all other young women in my community.

It was therefore fulfilling to be in the Coady in 2017 where every failure counted in a person's success. Through having faith in a tomorrow not built solely on lost times, I was ready to explore opportunities that would propel me to greatness, because "a river is never the same." While I am still on that journey, I am happy it is paying off as I continue to offer my unflinching support to the National Women's Council, presenting responsive constitutional amendment proposals, and developing gender policies and resolutions that make women partners in development.

I subsequently developed a leadership trait focused on building grassroots power, respecting diversity and being inclusive. The challenge to learn by exploring my beliefs, stories, perceptions and principles made me re-think stereotypical and discriminatory practices against vulnerable groups. I started working towards being more conscious of the intersectional traits of those I work with. This led me to be part of several campaigns and movements focused on emancipating minority groups, from the United States to Ghana, aimed at promoting social justice.

Home and Away Again
After graduating from the Coady I chose Pennsylvania State University for their unique master's degree in Labor and Global Workers Rights to continue my learning journey. This decision meant

committing more time, material and human resources to see this dream materialized. It also meant a tough decision to leave my four-year-old daughter and seven-year-old son who had been cared for by my late mother. I kept reminding myself of the importance of sacrificing to be different amongst the lot. It could not have been possible without the support of my mentors within the union movement in Ghana, my spouse and sisters who believed in my dreams.

With totally different approaches towards teaching and learning in Ghana and the United States, my stay at the Coady bridged the differences and trained me to be an analytical and critical thinker. Arriving at Penn State the academic program looked good, but the living conditions at the state college did not coincide with my stipend as a research assistant. I took a job as a cook at a hotel on campus for 10 hours a week, and cooked intermittently for students and residents who ordered food from my kitchen for a fee.

As difficult as it all seemed, I also enrolled in a minor in Adult Education against my advisor's advice. He was concerned I might not be able to deal with the workload. I knew I could do it because of the resilience I had built from my life experiences at the Coady. During very tough moments, I always counted on remembering the good feelings I got connecting with nature that I learned from the Mi'kmaq Indigenous leaders who had shared their knowledge with us. I knew since I had survived the traumas during that time, and developed more skills, I could succeed at Penn State.

The months at Penn State went by quickly. As an activist, I joined several organizations on campus including the Pan African Professional Alliance (PANAPA) which led me to joining several actions after the police shooting of Osagie Osazie in March 2019. My participation led to my delivering a speech at a vigil held in Osagie's honour. Many were worried about my safety in associating with the Black Lives Matter campaigns as an international student; others advised me to stay away from any such activity. To me however, being human and guaranteeing justice for myself and others in the future was far more important than being afraid to act.

As part of the program requirement at Penn State, students were required to do an internship with a social justice organization or trade union movement. I was lucky to be offered a place at the Solidarity

Center (SC) of the American Federation of Labor - Congress of Industrial Organizations (AFL-CIO) in Washington, DC. This rare opportunity contributed to building my career and networks. Working in the Africa department, I was tasked with doing research on the African Continental Free Trade Agreement (ACFTA) and helping to organize an international labor forum in Ghana. Ghana had been chosen for the celebration of the Year of Return worldwide in 2019 in recognition of the 400th year since slavery began.

Returning Home

Even though I had countless opportunities to stay in the United States, I was convinced coming home to Ghana would benefit many more, and help in challenging the systems of oppression that discriminated against women and girls.

It started with the story of a young lady harassed for wearing a hijab to an exam center on September 7th, 2019. This story propelled me to act swiftly. I remembered how weeks earlier I had personally experienced a similar act at the Kumasi airport on my way to Accra. A gentleman had insisted I could not complete boarding formalities without taking off my hijab. After asking him why I could not, using the 1992 Constitution and other international protocols, I was left alone. I wondered, what happens to other victims who cannot defend themselves to uphold their right to wear the hijab? Reading the story of the helpless girl challenged me to want to take action. I set out with others to fight for the liberation of Muslim women and girls against discrimination and marginalization for wearing a hijab.

We launched a campaign on September 11th, 2019, dubbed #hijabisanidentity, which sought to free Muslim women and girls from all forms of discrimination, marginalization and harassment. The campaign employed several strategies including organizing a town hall meeting, embarking on media engagements, developing digital messages, and a protest organized for October 12th, 2019. The protest was the first of its kind in Ghana, concurrently organized in three major cities in three regions: Accra in the Greater Accra Region, Kumasi in the Ashanti Region and Tamale in the Northern Region. It was a groundbreaking protest led by feminists with support from the Muslim Caucus in Parliament, the Office of the National Chief

Imam, the National Council of Zongo Chiefs. There were more than 10,000 protesters with massive coverage from local and international media houses like BBC, DW and Aljazeera.

Even though we encountered resistance from other Muslims with the use of the word 'choice' in our campaign, the grassroot power we built was enough to make people accept we had a legitimate point of view. Not considered a hijabi (a woman or girl who chooses to respectfully wear a head covering) myself, the opposition from other Muslims was that the hijab is compulsory according to the Holy Quran, and that I did not have the range of experience to lead the movement and campaign. A unique aspect of the campaign was the introduction of #hijabthursdays which saw people of other faiths sharing pictures of themselves in hijab. Subsequently, the protest led to several actions being taken by institutions such as the Social Security and National Insurance Trust Fund (SSNIT), Ghana Health Service (GHS), Mental Health Authority (MHA), West African Examination Council (WAEC), and many others.

My inspiration and motivation to lead the hijab campaign and others had come from the years of mentorship I received as a member of NETRIGHT and the Women's Manifesto Coalition of Ghana. The 15 years of mentorship started when I was a student leader, shaping my life and ways of doing things with the skills, knowledge and capacity development I received.

My Actions as a Way of Life
Since the #hijabisanidentity movement, which is still in existence, we have been engaged in other gender justice actions, including cyber activism on gender-based violence and why it is dangerous for media houses to centre men in discussions. We recently started a campaign on property ownership and women's rights in marriage due to the increasing mistreatment of Muslim women in marriage during divorce processes and on the demise of their spouses. This was after we supported a Muslim woman to get justice after a terrible divorce, which left her with nothing and no access to her children. Through the International Federation of Female Lawyers, we secured her access to her children and the husband was required to establish a profitable business venture for her.

I continue to speak on issues that affect and hinder women's progress in all spheres of life as a panelist and guest on several platforms. I consult and volunteer with several other organizations in the fight against inequality in all its forms. I was recently appointed as the Community Engagement Director for FemInStyle Africa magazine, and both as a council member and a fellow of the Centre for Social Justice (CSJ) in charge of the gender and social inclusion pillar. CSJ is a thinktank that does research and policy analysis, and offers other services towards a just nation for all Ghanaian citizens. To protect the interests of women workers from the claws of capitalist exploitation which squeezes blood out of their quest to survive, I continue to work as the gender equality officer of the General Agricultural Workers Union. My work focuses on ensuring that collective agreements, policies and legislation are responsive to the needs of all categories of workers. I run people-centred training programs and campaigns for workers, especially women and children, on diverse issues that guarantee decent work. To expose the predicament women workers are facing due to the COVID-19 pandemic, I started using my journalistic skills to write articles on the impact of the pandemic on women's employment, safety and health, with a call to action for stakeholders to protect their social and economic rights in Ghana. All of my articles critique the failure of legislative frameworks, policies and interventions of the state and make recommendations to provide adequate protection for vulnerable groups. As my dream of defeating inequalities between different classes and genders, and the struggle for a violence and sexual harassment free world lingers on, I continue to be offered platforms in Ghana and beyond to discuss my work and to critique policies, interventions and legislation that widen and entrench the inequality gap.

I know my promise to my advisor at Penn State to use my journalistic and other acquired skills from the Coady to liberate many has just begun. I will continue to commit to the emancipation of vulnerable groups through organizing, communication, advocacy and campaigns to demand action from the government of Ghana to protect women's livelihoods, sexual and reproductive rights; to end rape and rape culture, sexual harassment and gender-based violence; and to promote women's leadership at all levels.

Through the River of Life exercise at the Coady, I saw how the support of others had paved the way for my existence, made me appreciate my own contributions to my journey and accept that failure can be a bridge. I also understood that everyone's story is valid and can contribute to changing the world positively if shared.

I have internalized the principle that being a leader means making difficult choices, including risking one's life as necessary to achieve social justice. With the belief that "opinions build walls and stories build bridges," I hope my story will inspire you to change lives by challenging structural inequalities.

Endnotes

1   Coady, M.M. (1939). Masters of their Own Destiny: The story of the Antigonish Movement of adult education through economic cooperation. New York, NY: Harper & Brothers.

Three

My dream: Peace in rural schools in Kenya

Maina Wambugu Sebastian, Kenya

"I went to bed hungry many nights as a child. It was a Dream that dressed me up when I was ragged, and it was a Dream that filled me up when I was hungry. Now it's my Dream to see that no child in this world ever goes hungry … We can do better…we must!"

Dolly Parton[1]

I was a poor boy raised by a struggling mother in a rural slum area of Kenya. This is an area where patriarchy is valued, and mothers are faced with endemic societal stigma. My mother raised us single handedly from casual jobs she did on other people's farms. She could barely raise a dollar per day and when she got it, that meant gold to our household. It meant food on the table that day. Going to school was a luxury, eating a single meal each day was a miracle. Sleeping with an empty stomach was the norm. I remember days that my mother would hurriedly wake us up in the middle of rainy nights to push our bed to one of the corners of our tiny house to avoid pouring rain from leaking on us. I hated rainy season! Yet nothing denied me peace of mind more than going to school without adequate school fees or no school fees at all, spending a day with an empty stomach, with no textbooks to read. We trekked six kilometers daily to and from school. My mother could not afford a single pair of shoes, not even the ones made of old rubber tires by the Maasai or Kamba communities. Yet together with a group of community women, they contributed what little they could afford to support my education up to the college level.

The hardships I went through, the hard labour my mother did to raise us, the sleepless nights that I spent on an empty stomach and the inspiration that my mother constantly gave and demonstrated to me, ignited my dreams to promote peace at rural schools and in the community. I wanted to ensure that children never had to go through

what I went through. There can never be peace of mind when a child
has nothing to eat. A child can never understand, concentrate on
learning or complete schooling in an environment where food is a
rare commodity.

Lacking food is torturous. With hunger, growing children cannot
be motivated to go to school. They cannot concentrate in class and
learning cannot be fun. A child cannot be creative, and the mind
cannot operate efficiently when the stomach is empty. My idea to join
an agricultural college was motivated by the desire to help farmers so
they could grow some food for themselves and their families. Hunger
pains are hard to bear. I needed the skills to help families provide
adequate food for all community members.

My initial dream was to generate enough food for my mother and the
community at large. This inspired me to be an agronomist — an idea
incubated at an early age based on my own experience of hunger growing up. I vowed to do everything I could to ensure children and women
were not subjected to extreme hunger, conflict, and disrupted learning.

Food, water and pasture scarcity are catalysts for conflict among
people and communities who live side by side in our region of Kenya.
Escalation of such conflicts is complex when one community is pastoralist and nomadic, while the other practices agriculture. I was not
aware at a young age why my mother and others were so poor, and
why there was always conflict between the agriculturalists and pastoralists. It was later I understood that scarcity leads to competition,
and competition for scarce and diminishing resources such as land,
water and pasture leads to immeasurable conflicts and untold sufferings. And in such cases, it is the children who suffer most.

An American political scientist, Samuel P. Huntington, explained
that in the post-Cold War era, people's cultural and religious identities will mean conflicts will be based on scarcity of resources such as
water and food. War and conflict will no longer be between countries, but about cultures and resources.[2]

Starting with Peace in Community Development

In the presence of conflict or war, peace is disrupted and when peace is
absent there can be no learning, development and progress in general.
Conflicts lead to increased infections and diseases, low literacy levels,
deaths, hunger and famine. This was my experience growing up. Hence,

I knew peace was a precondition to the progress of our civilization.

To respond to this realization, I founded Youth Action for Rural Development (YARD) as a community based grassroots organization in 2002 after my training as an agronomist. Over the years YARD has assisted thousands of youth, children and women through several integrated initiatives. In a community where people are in constant competition for food, water and education, while at the same time fighting substance and drug use, YARD promotes peaceful coexistence among diverse people and helps build peace from within. YARD faithfully has supported over 350 students through college education. This boosted education in the region immensely. Those supported through YARD have come back to the community, are giving back, and are motivating other young people who are facing challenges they had previously encountered. The stories of positive change are numerous.

Over the years, YARD has been able to promote peace in all the communities where projects have been running. Peace prevails in a family where drug abuse does not occur, food is available, children continue going to school and communities are not competing for the little resources that are available.

The Dream – Promoting Peace at Rural Schools

In 2010, I had an opportunity to study Development Leadership at the Coady International Institute at St Francis Xavier University. For close to one year during my study, I had a lot of time to interact with international students. Most of them were educators and development practitioners with vast experiences, spanning the whole world. Equipped with the new learning and knowledge gained at the Coady and the interactions with other participants, I knew exactly what to do once I returned to my country.

After establishing YARD Kenya, and overseeing its growth as a learning organization, working on AIDS Control, and establishing a vocational school for training girls, I still felt there was something missing, something I still wanted to do. It was then that we decided to establish a peace school to directly provide competency-based education to children, feed them and help them resolve conflicts between their communities.

The idea of establishing a peace school was motivated by my own past experiences. When you grow up in an exceedingly difficult and toxic environment, such harsh reality triggers your mind and builds your resilience. All those difficult experiences I recounted earlier meant there was no peace in my early life. Once when my fountain pen went dry, I knew I would be in trouble with my teachers, because it meant I could not take any notes. I quickly got some green leaves and pounded them together with some pink flowers and made ink! I made something new! It had a colour no one had ever seen before: it resembled khaki. Both the other pupils and my teacher were amazed that I had invented a new way to make ink and a new colour!

Maruge Peace School was established to teach life skills to children and to promote peace between two bordering communities; both are poor. The children would learn to become agents of peace and reconciliation. The Maruge Peace School sits on a boundary between two communities. One is in Kiambu region where most people are farmers, while in Kajiado most people practice pastoralism. Years of hostility have built up towards each other; it is indeed a place where peace was needed. The choice of putting the peace school between these two communities was strategic and carefully thought out. Although the physical features of both communities are pretty much the same, the administrative and political boundaries between the two contributed to the division both communities felt.

Over decades there has been frequent conflict between the two communities. When animals from one community cross over to farms and destroy crops, it leads to serious problems. Farmers whose crops have been destroyed by animals would retaliate by crossing over into the other county where the pastoralists are, looking for the animals that ate the crops, and sometimes harming animals that were not involved. The conflicts always left an aftermath of mass destruction, houses burnt down, fields of crops destroyed, animals killed or maimed and sometimes lives lost. Many people must nurse wounds caused during the conflict. Women and children suffer most, and the effects of such conflicts are long term.

My dream is to promote peace in rural schools. The Maruge Peace School is a strategic attempt to be part of the solution towards peace-building through children and education. I brought a team of young people together that had gone through college and were looking for work. The jobs they were searching for were not forthcoming. My request to them was that they could be doing something more with their knowledge and education. I convinced them doing something for the children and the surrounding community would be easier and give more satisfaction than moving from one office to another. I am glad I still work with many of those initial volunteers!

In the wake of conflicts, children suffer extensively. My own family was internally displaced as were families we knew and had lived with for years. Hence, we made the decision to strategically locate and establish Maruge Peace School on the boundary between the two communities. YARD continues to be active, passing important life skills on to children from both communities, and providing access to basic health services, scholastic materials, environmental skills, talent building and psychosocial support.

The name of the school was inspired by an old man named Kimani Maruge, who went to grade one at the age of 84 years. He had missed out on going to school during the clamour for Kenya's independence, and again missed out when the government introduced fees for basic education. A change in government years later and a declaration of free basic education gave a chance for Kimani Maruge to join elementary school! He is in the Guinness Book of Records as the oldest pupil to have joined elementary school. He later died of a pneumonia-related illness after staying out in the cold at the Internally Displaced Persons (IDP) camp, which had been set up when political violence erupted. That violence has now turned tribal, and communities that had once lived together in peace have become enemies. How can all this be changed?

Children have clean hearts that do not harbour hate. They can be unaware of conflicts and tribalism, and can act as agents to promote and build peace in the region and in their communities. Children at the Maruge Peace School have built harmony and demonstrated this through joint activities such as planting trees in both communities and having regular communal meetings. Also, major celebrations happen when individual trees are planted on children's birthdays and we have a tree planting party. The school now sits amidst a forest of trees, each tree marking the birthdays of the children who planted them. The children take care of the trees and flowers by themselves and watch as they grow. The children are growing as well, and as they watch the trees grow, they understand what it means to grow up in a healthy peaceful environment. It is during this "outside" learning that children develop many other skills they are unlikely to learn while inside the walls of a classroom. The children feed chickens and their chicks, care for goats and their kids, water trees and trim their branches, take care of the soil, build healthy relationships and reconnect with nature. This kind of all-round education will have endless benefits and each day the children learn something new! Because agriculturalist and pastoralist children are learning together, they are learning to appreciate all these important aspects of living together and making sustainable livelihoods through well informed decisions and actions.

During conflict animals also suffer. They are maimed, killed, stolen or end up in the slaughterhouses. In return, the community whose animals have been stolen seeks revenge. They damage maize fields, vegetable fields, bananas, fruit trees, and burn houses. Children at the peace school learn the importance of each crop, each animal, contribute towards taking care of them, and learn the cultural attachment that the crops and animals hold for the different communities. For example, they get to know that if you take the cows away from the Maasai community, you are denying several families their livelihood and it can take several years for them to recover. Without cows you deny children milk, the blood they consume, manure for the fields, and you deny Maasai women who milk the animals the chance to sustain their families. This totally disrupts the communal ecosystem. The same learning will help the Maasai children to understand that if you destroy crops, you are promoting loss of livelihoods for several families and they become food insecure. Thinking of the children as future decision makers, this is the best time to help them learn about different cultures and how to make appropriate and well thought out decisions and actions in everyone's best interests to create peace. Maruge Peace School does this with precision.

Children, together with the teachers, visit several villages in both communities to deeply understand how the two different communities live. They come to understand they can live together even when there are differences in many aspects of their lives.

Maruge Peace School is an example of how education and children can promote peace between two communities in conflict. It is also a clear demonstration that children copy so much of what they see happening around them, or what they have been told by their seniors. Their behaviour is based on what they see! It is a great joy to see children change the behaviour of their generation, create peace and enjoy what so many others lacked at a young age. Having access to food, clothes, education, health and shelter is a fundamental right of all children, and is the responsibility of everyone who cares about the future generation. Over the years the approach of the school has demonstrated its efficacy in conflict resolution and promoting peace.

Peace takes Persistence and Sustained Commitment
Maruge Peace School has accomplished much and has not always been on a simple path. Even as I write this essay about peace, new conflicts were sparked between the two communities. In 2020, there was a minor conflict between Maasai and Kikuyu communities after Maasai animals crossed over the border and destroyed crops of the Kikuyu people. Tension escalated when members of Kikuyu community confiscated animals, and demanded compensation before releasing the captured animals. A swift call by the local leaders of both communities led to the decision to have a conflict resolution meeting at Maruge Peace School. The school was seen as a strategic meeting place for both communities because of its location, and because children from both communities were learning there. They became part of the solution and their appeal was loud and clear. They wanted peace! It was also the place where some families had come to take refuge from the conflict. To maintain and ensure constant peaceful coexistence, Maruge Peace School continues to create uniting activities such as planting trees, storytelling, game playing and parents exchange programs within the school and the villages. Through the children, as agents of peace, both communities will hopefully continue to embrace each other, bringing peace and reconciliation amongst themselves.

The Dream is not Complete, It Continues!
My dream is now to replicate the Maruge Peace School project. We want to reach as many children as possible and build initiatives to promote peace and resolve conflicts. The community safety net is being built by educating and supporting the children and ensuring their voices of peace are heard loudly in the region.

Endnotes

1   Parton, Dolly. (2013). Dream More: Celebrate the dreamer in you. New York, NY: Riverhead Books.

2   Huntington, S.P. (1996). The Clash of Civilizations and Remaking of World Order. New York, NY: Simon and Schuster.

— Four —

We are the story, we are the solutions: Building solidarity

Ehab Gamal, Egypt

"Everyone has the right, individually and in association with others, to promote and to strive for the protection and realization of human rights and fundamental freedoms at the national and international levels."

United Nations Declaration on
Human Rights Defenders, Article 1.[1]

Awakening the Activist Within

I was very young when I woke up to the concept of human rights and it was quite by accident.

I grew up in one of the largest informal settlements in my country. As a child, I had a stammer and became introverted. I felt ashamed every time I talked, so I stayed quiet. This meant I had very little interaction with other children and young people in my neighbourhood. I spent a lot of time alone.

When I was 15 years old, my older sister was working as a teacher with people with disabilities in a neighbourhood association. One day, she forgot something at home and called me to bring it to her. When I arrived, a child named Anter, a young person with Down Syndrome, immediately started talking to me and introducing me to all his friends with similar disabilities. He did not care about my stuttering speech, nor did his friends. He didn't wait for me to take the first step in getting to know him and his friends, he just jumped in! Anter pushed me to join the artistic activities they were doing. As a loner, I had not done these activities before, nor anything like them. At the end of the day, Anter told me the weekly activities schedule and said he would see me next time. I continued to go back and participated in these activities and discovered talents I didn't know I had!

Through the association, I began participating in seminars and training about the rights of people with disabilities, as well as children's rights. It was during that time I began to wake up and realize how many human rights violations were being experienced by people living in slum areas.

Since then, I have been trying to live more like Anter and honour the awakening he ignited in me: to create spaces that accept people as they are; enable them to discover themselves and their interests; seek to integrate them into their community; and, change the current situation so that communities, especially slum neighbourhoods, can fully access their human rights.

With my new awareness, I worked to form different youth groups. In one group, we decided to create a youth space in our neighbourhood, where youth could practice their hobbies, build their identities and implement initiatives of their own making. We met challenges, such as being rejected by the established associations, who had their own youth programs. We didn't give up; we carried out many activities and community initiatives with children and youth in the neighbourhood, toward this goal of establishing our own youth center.

Since then, I have been a director and organizer of non-profit organizations for youth empowerment, which is an expression of my commitment to just social development and inclusive change. Doing youth work led me into working in community, and then in civil society. It led me to obtain a bachelor's degree in Law and a diploma in Civil Society and Human Rights. I also studied governance, transparency and accountability, community facilitation and youth leadership with the Coady International Institute.

Around the same time, the Arab Spring was blowing across North Africa. Like many youth, I participated in political movements that sought to achieve the fundamental goals and principles of the revolution: "Bread, Freedom, Human Dignity, Social Justice." I fully participated in the movement to seek these four basic rights and this had a tremendous impact on shaping who I am today. It strengthened my interest in working for the public good. It contributed to increasing my belief that real change can happen only by working simultaneously at both the political and social levels. The experience also opened a new horizon — I dreamt it was possible to change the situation in slums.

As well, I felt a greater sense of responsibility towards my country and the Arab world. I also have a debt of responsibility to those martyrs who paid with their lives, as the price for our dreams.

To complement my experience in the revolutionary movements, my studies in law, civil society and human rights helped me better understand the formal systems in our country. I learned there were legal ways for people to claim their rights. A fellowship in Youth Leadership for Civil Society helped me increase my understanding of the impact of NGOs in a country. Also, I deepened my learning about applying practical and participatory tools to strengthen citizen voice. I was surrounded by experiences that shaped me as a human rights activist.

It was around this time that I began to identify as a Human Rights Defender (HRD). I believe no real development can take place anywhere without brave HRDs fulfilling this duty to their societies. For HRDs, the collection and accessibility of information contributes to the understanding of societal conditions. When HRDs raise their voices with and for others, they are doing so because human rights are being denied or oppressed.

Working in Civil Society and Applying My Activist Knowledge
After the fellowship and time at the Coady, my work in civil society took many directions to promote participation, freedom of expression, and basic rights for communities and for groups that suffer from marginalization and social exclusion. In my slum community, which has more than 650,000 citizens, I developed and participated in many innovations to create spaces for community participation and development. We were suffering from too few basic services and too many violations of basic human rights. Some of those innovations included:

Rights of Persons with Disabilities, Creating Inclusive Spaces: In one local community development NGO for the rights of people with disabilities, I worked to create inclusive social and youth spaces in diverse communities. I also volunteered as co-founder and member of the management board for another organization focused on the rights of persons with disabilities. This organization's goal is to assimilate people with disabilities into their community and empower them to advocate and mobilize for their social causes. The NGO works to build communal awareness of the rights of people with disabilities, within the laws of the land, and to give legal assistance to fully access these rights.

Cultural Space and Theatre: Establishing a cultural space and theatre, with the efforts of volunteers and three civil society organizations working in the field of culture, confirmed my belief in art and culture as an important approach to social change. We tried and were successful. A theatre was built from recycled materials and was open to all. At least two performances were presented monthly. All performances incorporated elements of the Theatre of the Oppressed[2] and Egyptian theatre scenes with singing to revive Egyptian cultural heritage. They were created and performed by professional artists, with young people and children from the neighbourhood. The public was invited free of charge.

Youth-led Co-operative Learning Hub: Because of my experiences in setting up different youth spaces and learning from these efforts, I participated with others to create and support a youth-led co-operative learning hub. It was registered as an Egyptian NGO and provided meeting space, a learning community, networking platform and coaching program for youth-led development initiatives that bring ideas and dreams alive in their communities. We took an organic approach; that is, everyone owns the organization. Our mission was to support youth-led initiatives and groups that have an idea or dream by providing learning, coaching and networking to contribute in their personal development and their communities' development.

Safe Spaces for Collective Learning: Beyond my community, we established an NGO initiative among three groups aimed at empowering youth by creating a safe space for collective learning, enabling them to mobilize their resources and to respond to challenges and aspirations. We believed change can happen through volunteering, building youth leaders and focusing on education, arts and economic empowerment. Our development model was documented as an approach for establishing youth NGOs in slum neighbourhoods that suffer from marginalization and social exclusion.

Movement for Human Rights in Egypt: During my political participation in the revolution, we co-founded a mass action committee. I was responsible for the work committees in southern Cairo, created to support the people's struggle for radical reforms. The intention was to re-distribute wealth for the benefit of the poor and low income families, and to build a democracy of popular participation. The Movement defended the demands to achieve the call for "Bread, Freedom, Dignity and Social Justice." It also sought to resist suppression by military power, authoritarianism, violence and sectarianism. Due to the narrowing civil society, the closure of public life and the arrest of many of the Movement's leaders and members, the Movement has stopped functioning.

The Change We Seek Can Happen Everywhere: Two years after the revolution, I was working in an international organization. Colleagues from the same organization in other countries often visited Egypt. I found it easy to talk with one colleague about everything — the situation of youth in Egypt, the revolution. I remember telling him, "I want to see change in every neighbourhood, to see it happen everywhere." He didn't say anything or show any expression on his face. Six months later, his home office invited me to visit and discuss these same ideas and to write a project proposal together.

When I returned to Egypt, for a number of reasons, I had to leave the organization. I refocused my energy into the associations and spaces I had helped set up as a volunteer. My friendships with my international colleagues continued. I would ask for their opinion and advice about the work I was doing and whenever they visited Egypt, we would meet.

Consequences of Social Activism

Soon, because of my work and political and social activism, my life in Egypt became endangered. I wrote to friends outside the country, told them what was happening and how the situation was now getting dangerous for me. I asked their advice. Everyone thought for my safety that I should leave Egypt quickly. Arrangements were made immediately and within just seven hours I took flight from Egypt.

Once the decision was made to go, I had to keep travelling for six months which took me to three countries and nine cities. I was not ready for all of this moving around. I thought there would be some months of traveling, and then the situation in Egypt would calm down and I would return. It's been more than three years now and this hasn't happened.

My friends worked on solutions to get me into their country. It took lots of paperwork to obtain a visa, which turned out to be only a three month solution. Since then, three months has been extended to one year and seven months. Nothing about the situation is clear. We really can't get a full picture of the situation I face, and we continue to look for alternatives that might work for me.

We looked at the legal aspects for me being in this country or going elsewhere. We looked for solutions consistent with our values. They introduced me to friends in the city and strived to create a network of relationships around me. They helped find me a place to live and provided support at work. They consistently helped me understand the context and work style in their country, which is very different from the context at home.

We dance together, maybe not enough, and that helps me defeat the waves of depression and stress that I struggle with and helps me find the energy to continue. They bear with me through all the persecution, legal restrictions and social conditions faced by anyone who was not born here as a white, blond boy with wealthy parents. Through all of this, they help me see the beautiful, true face of their country. Certainly, they make me feel like this country could be my second home and that they are my family. Everyone tries to help me — giving me support, reminding me to wear warm clothing, to take vitamin D and even changing the language of the meeting so I can participate equally. My friends are amazing. Every sentence is full of "Don't worry — we'll find a solution or you can contact me any time." They say these words and they mean it. They stick to their word, and follow through.

Over the past three years, every political and social activist in every country or city I have been in has supported me. This support has given me extra days to live in this life. I had many accidents during my life, especially during the revolution years. I often wonder why I haven't died already and why I'm still alive. I don't know the answer to this, but I'm convinced there is still time for me; time to try again; time to prevent the killing of another person; to open up new spaces where everyone can express themselves; where the rights of all are respected and appreciated; where everyone can play and dance as they want, without any fear; and, where we can all live together as human beings.

So, I left my home country, and I'm still alive. I don't know how or why my life is saved. I do know that I have won some extra time and I want to try again — for the many, many who died and didn't get the chance. Most HRDs face similar dangers and more, yet they continue because we are seeking the same things. They continue to defend their rights and the rights of others around them. There are others who, because they are afraid of facing the consequences alone, will take a stand against their own beliefs. And there are still others, more vulnerable than me, who deserve another opportunity to do more.

Is There a Limit to What We Can Ask of Friends?
I hassle myself by worrying about whether my friends think I have used our friendship when I faced problems. As part of this essay, I decided to ask some of them why they supported me and whether they felt used. Here are some excerpts of what they said:

"I knew about the commitment you had as a HRD on the streets and how you combined that with community development work with youth. When I learned of your situation and your desire to continue your work, it seemed that getting away for a while was the best thing for you to do. For your future, it made sense to support whatever people were doing to support you."

"One of David Korten's suggestions for 'getting to the 21st century' (which I think is still relevant today) is to support individual leaders for 'who they are and who they may be' not for 'what they do or could do in the future.' Just giving support to individuals who put their heart and spirit into 'being' creators of just world is a good 'investment'."

"I never felt our friendship was being used or abused, quite the opposite. We offered to help in any way we could because we trusted and respected you, and your work as a human rights defender. And still do."

"I was honoured and humbled when you called upon us. In fact, I never recall being asked or felt I was being asked for anything. I heard a well-articulated story from you of feeling trapped and directionless. There were wonderful indicators of fearlessness."

From these types of responses, I consider it wise for all HRDs to know the support they receive is based on the relationships they have built in their community or organization. Call on these people. If they are friends, they will not feel used because they know you. As friends they can say no. Some will be willing and even want to do more than you ask.

When I talk to organizations about building a program to support

HRDs under threat, it will be important to remind them that people help because they know the person. Questions of what kind of support is needed are a helpful starting place.

For HRDs who leave their home country without anything, you have to be ready to ask for support from others, which is not always easy, but you will have to do it to survive.

For HRDs its important to build good relationships based on openness — be honest with people, even if it takes courage. For the people who know you, don't hide anything from them. Build trust by telling the truth, even if they may not approve of all your actions. Know that once you lie, then people can't trust you and they will stop listening to you. For an HRD in exile, especially political exile, you will face many risks. So always tell it like it is; nothing is lost and much are gained by always being honest with people.

During the COVID-19 pandemic in 2020, trying to secure legal status as an immigrant/visitor in another country was hard. Trying to get a visa or a passport renewed was time consuming with little co-operation from program administrators. Months passed without making any progress in securing my status as a legal visitor/immigrant!

Solidarity is really important. When people stand with you, be ready to stand with other HRDs. Because of everything that I have been through, I want to send a message to all HRDs everywhere to tell them, "We are with you, we feel you, we are afraid with you of dangers you face, and we will take risks with you." It's time to create a safety net available to all HRDs as the true face of solidarity. Through such a safety net or permission to rest, HRDs won't have to struggle alone. Supportive organizations require a model to protect those who fight to achieve human rights for all. Because we believe in solidarity, we can all be ourselves and join in.

Call to Action for Solidarity with HRDs

Here are some ideas inspired by friends who have provided different forms of support that helped me during times of danger and risk. These actions would be helpful to political and social activists in every country I have been in during the last three years.

A Safety Net or Permission to Rest plan is a mechanism that could be put in place to support all HRDs. The values of such a program of solidarity for HRDs would include justice, freedom of expression and opinion, and sharing personal and collective risk and responsibility.

An HRD Database built to help create a common understanding of what is happening could reduce attacks against HRDs. Such a database of the people working in the field of human rights in various countries could document and map the status of HR violations and risks HRDs face at the community and project level. Project staff would meet with law enforcement authorities to share the project and the role of HRDs, and discuss the importance of the legal protection.

Training in Awareness, Skills and Tools to support HRDs will be vital. Such a training package for youth in communities and organizations could include videos on who is an HRD, how to protect yourself as an HRD, peaceful dialogue and conflict resolution, risks HRDs face, power analysis and reporting mechanisms for violations, digital security, and the UN Declaration on HRDs. This training could be offered annually.

Supporting Communities that Host HRDs will be important. This support could be in the form of establishing work programs, networking with other activists to share experiences, learning and resources. The integration of HRDs into rehabilitation and employment programs is also an important form of support. Policies must be established that provide a legal framework to report cases of violations against HRDs and a guide to supporting HRDs at risk.

Training to Strengthen Civil Society would include the following: digital and communication security; encryption tools and services to protect private communications from surveillance; local funding from civil society through partner associations and local funding sources; and using the CIVICUS[3] Monitor to build knowledge about the risks faced by civil society and the HRDs in particular countries.

A Safe Exit Gate is an important emergency support mechanism. This would include a direct communication channel for quick response to an HRD at risk — an emergency hotline/email in every country with trained people to monitor the lines. HRDs who face risks would always have someone to call.

An HRD Emergency Fund could be set aside in an umbrella organization to respond to emergency situations faced by HRDs. As a direct resource to HRDs to help ensure their safety, it could be used for legal fees for those being judicially harassed; for medical fees for those who have been attacked or suffer a medical condition; for family assistance for imprisoned HRDs or family members who are at risk; and for travel within or outside the country toward temporary relocation to escape dangerous situations or continuous persecution. This could be in the form of a fellowship, internships, work, workshops, study, and/or sponsorship programs. Based on the commitment to leave no HRD behind, civil society organizations' staff could donate one day of wages per year to the fund. This fund could support those who fight for a common purpose, as well as funding civil society projects that support HRDs on the front lines. Financial support for these activities has a basis in friendships.

My Hopes for Returning to My Home, My Community
My hope is to one day return to my home, my community and continue my community work. In preparation for this, I want to create a comprehensive model of development so that all inhabitants of communities in the slum areas can access their basic human rights. I want to develop an approach for activists with youth organizations about working with marginalized and socially excluded neighbourhoods. I want to continue to establish creative spaces and youth associations in all slum communities that suffer from marginalization. These are spaces for learning and participation of young people to work together to organize their communities. I dream of forming a network of slum youth that seeks to organize their communities to change the status of slums and contribute to dialogue and research that inform government development policies for slums. And I want to contribute to the role of culture and theatre in community spaces in marginalized neighbourhoods.

I want to thank all the friends for their support and solidarity over the past three years, as well as the reflection that has inspired this essay. We stand together.

Endnotes

1   "The Declaration on Human Rights Defenders, adopted by the General Assembly in its Resolution 53/144, is based on and incorporates human rights enshrined in legally-binding international instruments. The Declaration reaffirms rights that are instrumental to the defense of human rights, including, inter alia, freedom of association, freedom of peaceful assembly, freedom of opinion and expression, and the right to gain access to information, to provide legal aid and to develop and discuss new ideas in the area of human rights (see A/63/288, annex, para. 2)."
https://www.ohchr.org/EN/Issues/CivicSpace/Pages/
DeclarationHumanRightsDefenders.aspx

2 A description of Theatre of the Oppressed can be found on the website Acting Now:
http://actingnow.co.uk/what-is-theatre-of-the-oppressed/

3   "CIVICUS aims to share reliable, up-to-date data on the state of civil society freedoms in all countries. Their interactive world map allows access to live updates from civil society around the world, tracks threats to civil society and provides an opportunity to learn about the ways in which our right to participate is being realized or challenged."
https://humanrightsconnected.org/tag/data-visualization/

Five

Taking on leadership
to promote youth leadership

Suran Maharjan, Nepal

This essay is about a young development practitioner converting learning into action. From Nepal to studies in Canada and Italy, and professional work with Action Aid and VSO, I have had opportunities to learn and demonstrate my leadership skills to promote youth leadership. There have been challenges and successes along the way, but my willingness to step forward and take risks helped me learn a lot about leadership.

The Coady Journey

I'll start with my experience at the Coady International Institute in Antigonish, Canada. I became a participant of the 2009 *Diploma in Development Leadership*, the same year the Coady celebrated its 50th anniversary. I was 22 years old at that time, well below the average age of other participants. I was active and enthusiastic. I was told I was the second youngest ever to attend the Diploma Program. My participation in it and my entire Coady experience was simply amazing and full of learning, but it almost did not happen.

The Coady's *Diploma in Development Leadership Program* is designed for mid-career development professionals to reflect on and learn from their previous work experience. I was initially not selected for the program, because of my age and perceived lack of experience. I did not accept no for an answer. In consultation with my boss at the time, who was a Coady graduate herself, I appealed the decision and made a case for my involvement based on my experience as a youth volunteer, my great enthusiasm for learning, and potential for the future. Fortunately, I was reconsidered, admitted to the program and began a wonderful learning journey. I learned then that having a vision for what you want and working towards it with confidence and persistence can be rewarded. I also learned that asking for help to achieve your goal is important.

Soon after starting at the Coady, I wrote: "When I came to the Coady Institute I expected to learn from the courses. But what's most amazing is not only the courses but the way they are taught and the opportunity to learn from other people's experiences — leaders who are changing the context in their own countries. The whole Coady environment is very inspirational."

I was told the Coady is an ocean of opportunity and I witnessed the same. I was not only inspired by the rich experience facilitators brought to class, but also by the atmosphere at the Coady — one could find learning everywhere. My learning not only happened in class, but it was also in the comfort of the Marie Michael library, from the participatory activities, from friends at the main university and the spirit of my fellow participants who had rich experience to offer. It was an environment where I received support from facilitators and staff, and the perspectives of diverse people were valued. I realized I wanted to re-create this kind of inspiration and atmosphere of learning everywhere in my future career. As a young person this environment helped me to be creative, value the different perspectives of the team, look for solutions, and thrive by taking on new challenges and initiatives for social change.

During the Diploma Program, I opted to do independent research on using the web and social media for development. The term social media back then was still very new and research on social media for development was just starting. It was an area the Coady was just learning about as well. I knew there would be some risk in finding information in this new area, and having my conclusions accepted. I had some experience with social media as a youth networker in Nepal. I had been advocating for the importance of information and communication technologies (ICT) in the development sector, and the way social media can change our lives in the future. When I was showcasing an example of this reality, demanding that we could not ignore social media, it was still not seen as a priority by the Coady staff. This is not the case anymore; the rapid development of ICT and social media changed the way we communicate. Now social media is everywhere. I spent many long hours in the Coady and the university library, and at computers in the student union building. I was fully supported by my research supervisor Olga Gladkikh, who provided mentorship in such a new area and challenged me by her critical and constructive feedback. Providing such mentorship and challenge demonstrated another aspect of leadership. I learned to be persistent, self-critical and realized the importance of continuous learning. My research report was featured in a global knowledge portal in the same year, and I presented my research at a media conference in Kathmandu in 2010. This was a great boost to my confidence.

Before I left the Coady, I met with the Director Mary Coyle and discussed how the Coady needed to change to adapt to the new online world. I provided three suggestions to take forward: run specialization courses on new media, launch a web portal to connect with thousands of Coady grads, and offer more online courses. I remember her humbleness and inspiring nature. She heard my suggestions and thanked me for being honest. Her reaction and openness for critique were great examples of leadership and how to encourage the creativity of young people. I feel glad the Coady has since offered a certificate course on using social media for development, invested resources to connect graduates around the world and facilitated more courses online.

When I returned to Nepal, I used my knowledge and confidence to take on many initiatives in social media and ICT for development. I had cofounded a knowledge portal in 2008, **www.ixplore.info**, which was an online avenue to explore, share and connect with information, resources and opportunities in the development sector in Nepal. When it started it was the first of its kind in Nepal. I continued with it until 2013, and later in 2020 it was discontinued to make room for something new. Any intervention in ICT for development requires continuous updating and change. Though the portal was discontinued, the importance of social media in the development sector is now well established.

Master in Cooperation and Development
When I came back to Nepal, I was still hungry for learning opportunities. Luckily, I found a master's degree program run by the Institute for Advanced Studies at the University of Pavia in Italy. The focus of the course was economics, development economics, social science and project management. The degree required an internship

and a thesis so I thought the Coady would be the best place to do this. The internship as an Educational Program Associate helped me to connect intense knowledge of development economics with leadership. The opportunities for learning in the multicultural environment at the Coady also increased my confidence of working with diverse teams.

It was quite dramatic after my internship in the Coady when I came back to Nepal. I decided not to open my laptop and not to read anything including newspapers for a month! It was a conscious decision due to the overwhelming amount of reading and writing for my thesis. I was burnt out. I remembered how I crashed in the Coady library when chapters of my thesis were all over my mind. For internal peace, I often would take a YouTube break with my headphones. I did not notice that people were laughing at me as it was visible that my head was shaking with the rhythm of the music. Often, young development professionals tend to overdo it. Slowing down and taking a break is valuable. Learning is important, at the same time 'unlearning' and 'relearning' are equally important. Unlearning what you have already learned enables you to see things from a fresh perspective and open creative space in the mind. I needed a break from learning when I returned to Nepal, and realized a good leader must provide a space for unlearning and relearning.

Putting Learning into Action
Global Citizen Facilitator — ActionAid International Nepal: The rich experience of adult education pedagogy and the approach to participatory facilitation which I experienced at the Coady was phenomenal, and I was able to customize the approach at ActionAid International just a month after I returned to Nepal. I secured a position with them in a unique Global Citizens Course project. I was excited about this new challenge, although the job description was abstract. I was ready to take the risk and stepped up with energy, curiosity and enthusiasm for this opportunity. The Global Citizens Course is part of Global Platforms, a network for youth-led activism in ActionAid, that seeks to support various youth-led initiatives by capacity development and to promote young people as drivers of change towards a more just, sustainable and democratic world. The concept of learning in global platforms was inspired by Nikolaj F. S. Grundtvig (1783-1872), a Danish pastor, philosopher and teacher of

the Folk High School Movement, who followed principles of participatory methods, public action learning, political empowerment using a feminist lens, learning by doing and dreaming big.

Within the next few months, I designed and delivered the first edition of the course to youth from Nepal and Denmark. The four-month course covered areas such as understanding poverty and development, volunteering, project design and implementation, fundraising and living beyond the comfort zone. A month long study trip to India was built into the program where youth got to experience life beyond their borders.

During the course, I focused on promoting leadership opportunities for participants, as they had to design and deliver small projects. I saw their interventions as fully youth-led. Being a youth myself mentoring their intervention, I felt I was part of each intervention, just playing a different role. After each intervention, there was a detailed reflection conducted that created a space for youth to learn from each other. It is important to provide this space for youth and to promote their leadership. This makes youth independent and encourages them to look for solutions when they face challenges.

Ongoing Journey at VSO: My leadership journey of learning and engagement in the development sector continued, and with it new opportunities arose. In 2014, I moved to VSO as Project Co-ordinator of a development program called International Citizen Service (ICS) which focused on youth volunteering. The following year I became Project Implementation Manager in the same program. VSO is the global leader in promoting the Volunteering for Development approach. It has mobilized over 80,000 volunteers over 60 years. There my leadership skills were stretched once again and taken to a different level. My role was not limited to implementing the project, but also designing, managing and a level of accountability. I have now been on the management team in VSO Nepal since 2015. Currently, I manage the youth program in VSO Nepal where my focus is to strengthen the outcomes of youth programs by embedding quality youth engagement. In Nepal, 1,637 youth volunteers were mobilized between 2012 to 2020 in ICS projects. ICS volunteering programs are designed in a way to contribute to a positive impact in the community, while volunteers can develop their skills and become active citizens. They contribute to community development work and eventually go back to their own contexts with a new experience. In a nutshell, youth are challenged to change themselves to change their world.

Often youth are quickly motivated and get frustrated even faster. Youth provide opportunities for the nation to develop, but it is a huge challenge if their engagement is not addressed well. Youth engagement can be strengthened with a broad development approach, and partnership is key to achieving success. Establishing a strong partnership with the National Youth Council under the Ministry of Youth and Sports was very satisfying to me. The partnership promotes working for a wider sector, where marginalized youth are reached and their voices are heard. It helps minimize the frustration of the youths by providing enabling spaces and engaging opportunities. Recent engagement in the Voluntary National Review of the United Nations Sustainable Development Goals (SDG) which brought in marginalized youth voices also inspired me, as often their voices are left out. The SDGs cannot be achieved if youth are left behind.

While I was at the Coady, I took the *Learning Organization and Change* certificate course, facilitated by Debbie Castle and Balakrishna Venkatesh (Venky). The course mixed theory with a joint practical assignment. We were assigned to make a yellow page directory of the entire Coady class with lots of details. Our class was fully engaged in data collection and input. When we reached the design phase and finalization, due to the need for computer skills, only a few participants including me were involved. We worked day and night to create a publication, and our cohort celebrated the success. We had a reflection session and discussed that, even though the desired outcome was reached, those who were left out due to the skill gap didn't feel good about it. It was an eye-opening practical session for me! I realized it is not only important to reach the target; the process used to get there is equally important.

In my view VSO has all the characteristics of a learning organization. The environment is both pragmatic and inspirational. That is one key reason the past six years have gone so swiftly, as I have found new opportunities and challenges, and a learning culture that enables staff or volunteers to learn, grow and contribute to the vision of the organization, "A fair world for everyone." The organization is global, not only in its work around the world and historical footprint in many countries, but the way it connects all staff members. I have no barrier to reach any staff in any part of the world. I see a huge investment in creating an enabling learning environment. It gives a feeling of working in a real global organization. My leadership capacity has grown from self-reflection and the enabling environment created in every layer of the organization.

My Reflection on Leadership

It is not necessary to be a leader to practice leadership. Often a leader is perceived as a person who is in a high position in a formal work setting or in politics. If I had to choose between being a leader and leadership, I would prefer the latter. In my professional career in ActionAid and VSO, I have had the opportunity to work both as a team member and a leader for my functional unit. Also, in my early career in the development sector by co-founding a non-profit organization, Xplore International, I had the opportunity to take leadership into a new working area such as ICT and social media for development.

Below are learnings I have gained on my leadership journey. These may be useful to other young people exploring their own leadership.

Vision: I always have a vision for my work to guide me. The vision I have is intended to reach outcomes that contribute to the organization's broader vision; in a way it's a vision within a vision. I share this vision with the team to incorporate their ideas and create a shared vision. This approach helps me to articulate where and how I want initiatives to move forward. Most importantly my vision is not secret, abstract, and only in my mind. I deliberately make a space for discussion and reflection; I share my opinion and am also keen to listen to others' ideas. This helps build consensus among team members.

Inspiration: I feel a need to be inspired by others, and to inspire others. I am inspired by the dedication of people, their positive thinking, actions, learning attitude and aptitude, and vibe for change. I search for inspiration from the small things around me; for example, when youth share changes in the way they think and act after volunteering, and learning enhances the professional growth of team members. Inspiration fuels my passion and makes me eager to learn new things. I am also keen to inspire others by modelling leadership behaviours. I do this by various means including achieving results effectively and efficiently, consistently improving the way I work, expanding my knowledge and skills, taking challenges, showcasing innovations, being open to conversation and sharing positive vibes even in difficult situations.

I witnessed inspiration everywhere at the Coady. It was not only the veteran staff members and experienced participants who inspired us by their deep people-rooted conviction, but also the building itself — the hallway full of quotes, the photo mosaic, rich historical stories and the cozy library.

Learning Everywhere and All the Time: I see learning everywhere; the more I am challenged the more I learn. I think one needs to be open to learn new things. Something may be right today, but may not be right in future since contexts change, so unlearning is also important. I keep updated on my working themes and make efforts to adapt to the new context swiftly. Giving others the space to learn and helping them learn is also essential to promote a learning culture.

Team: Managing people is more of an art than a science of human resource principles. In my work experience, I have always considered my team as my strength. My persistent focus is to create an environment of trust, a reciprocal trust between me and my team. As the leader of a functional team, I believe my team intends to achieve the goals, therefore my approach is to let them decide their way of working. Whether a team member has many years of experience or is someone who has just started, they can contribute equally to the team. My role as a leader is to create a favourable environment for all members of the team to grow.

Moving In and Out of Leadership: There is one tendency in leadership that is common: "once a leader always a leader." In a work context "once the manager always the manager." I think there is something wrong with this concept. A leader should open spaces for others; that other person can be your follower or a person you manage in the work context. A youth naturally comes with newer knowledge and skills. Give them space. The concept of leadership is not dependent on the age of the person, rather on the capacity that person possesses. I do not limit myself or others and am open to new challenges all the time.

Taking Risks: In a normal setting there are established systems and processes. This tendency to business as usual needs to be changed as the context changes. However, changing any systems and processes will be challenging and can carry risks. As a leader, it is important to discuss any potential change and its potential impact, both positive and negative, before taking a risk. The risk-taking capability of an initiator is a key aspect of leadership. It is important to recognize there is no guarantee that decisions made while taking risks are going to be beneficial all the time; there can be negative consequences. The leader needs to look ahead and take a risk to achieve change. It is important for leaders to continuously challenge themselves to move beyond the concept of business as usual.

Innovation and Change: It is often challenging to define an innovation. In the development sector, is innovation an approach, a result, or both? Or is it new technology? In an organization, innovation is considered a crucial factor of success. If a leader is clear on a project's innovativeness, is ready to accept new things and adapt to the new context quickly, the change we are talking about can be achieved quickly. A leader should promote innovation in the organization and be ready to change as contexts change. Searching for innovation is also a key factor within myself. I believe one should always be thinking about what else is possible beyond what I'm doing now.

Stepping into Leadership as a Young Professional

I have been working in the development sector as a life-long learner who wants to contribute to change as a youth professional. I want to be inspired and hope to inspire others. Continuous reflection is a key aspect of what I do as a learner and a leader. The Coady experience had a lasting impact on me and other graduates, who connect and constantly reflect on their practice. I was always keen to learn beyond course content. I was consistently observing and reflecting on 'how' and 'why.' 'What' is usually obvious, but looking for a deeper understanding of an issue, searching for how and why are essential. These powerful questions make a young professional more insightful, self-reliant, and aware that learning is a lifelong process. This idea of learning everywhere matters to me; it helps me to take more risks and face challenges. I seek continuous change within myself and am keen to initiate an avenue for youth who have a desire to work for change and express leadership in their own contexts.

Six

Negotiating complexity as Coady graduates

Mary Ramsis, Egypt and Shaiju Chacko, India

Our association started at the Coady International Institute in 2011 as classmates in the *Diploma in Development Leadership*. We are Mary Ramsis, an Egyptian community development practitioner working in an international funding organization in Egypt; and Shaiju Chacko, a Catholic priest, working in Jammu and Kashmir, India. Ten years after completing the Diploma Program we have taken this precious opportunity to reflect upon our lives and work, and how the skills, knowledge and values acquired have shaped and influenced us.

In our cohort we were 49 people from 20 countries who became friends. Our class T-shirt aptly said, "Coady brings us together," a collective experience that influenced our lives in many significant ways. Two years later in 2013, the two of us met in India by coincidence and renewed our friendship. Despite few commonalities in

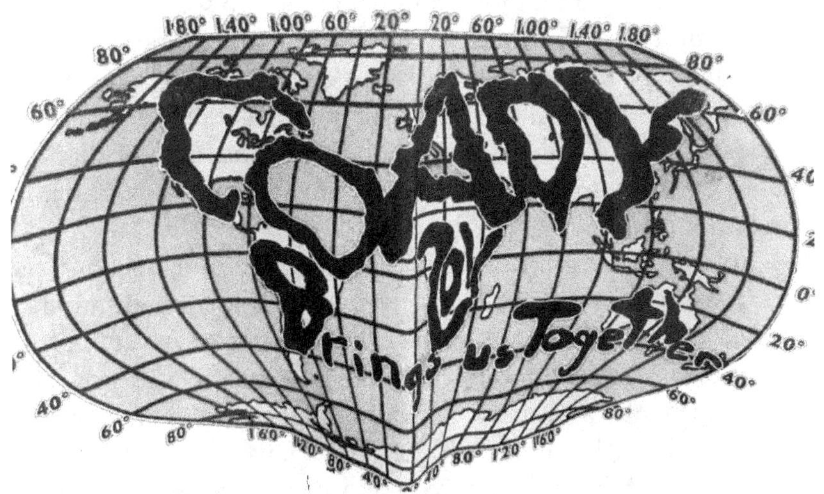

Picture 1: T-shirt logo created by the 2011 Class

language, culture, work interests, gender, we continue to experience a deep connection, making us co-travellers and friends. In this essay, we share some reflections of our parallel journeys as agents of change, and how we attempt to negotiate pathways in our respective complex, contextual realities. Our own multiple identities and the Coady experience remain the common reference points throughout this 10-year journey.

Building Relationship is the Key to Success

Mary: Shaiju, what comes to mind as the most remarkable experience you had after you returned from the Coady? And what made it remarkable?

Shaiju: When I returned, I was asked to lead a large and complex initiative to prepare youth of the Jammu and Kashmir valley to participate in the local and national economy. There were project stakeholders at all levels. We were asked to reach out to communities, local and state level religious leaders, State and Central Government officials and private sector companies to prepare them to absorb youth in their organizations. Most importantly, we were to engage young boys and girls in the project who had low trust in the system, little exposure to the job market, and often low confidence in themselves. We had an ambitious aim to reach 17,000 young people, train and prepare them to find jobs, and help them do so.

The community and youth mobilizations posed major challenges. As we started rolling out that initiative, one village at a time, block by block, covering 22 districts, organizing public gatherings, campaigning door-to-door, I realized it would be critical to approach local religious heads to generate positive opinions about the initiative in their communities.

Many of these areas in Kashmir are Muslim dominated, and mobilization work by a Catholic priest from a Christian organization, Don Bosco Tech (DB Tech), was tricky. We were successful in forging relationships through our local staff colleagues with the local masjid (mosque) committees. We even managed to get the project announced through the masjids, just after prayers.

In Jammu, a Hindu dominated region, we garnered the goodwill of the temple committees to hold public meetings inside temple spaces. I remember in Nagrota Gujroo in Kathua District, we were able to set up a training centre within the temple complex. We received all the necessary social and operational support from temple management, as well as the Trust which owned the building.

In Ladakh, which is primarily Buddhist, we approached the Ladakh Buddhist Association for support in identifying potential youth candidates. Besides providing legitimacy, this also gave the youth confidence to enrol in the project.

It was a remarkable experience for me because I realized the importance of finding allies who can positively influence an initiative and the course we were offering. The religious leaders, no matter what their affiliations, became allies in that noble objective of engaging young boys and girls in the project and supporting us in our ambitious venture.

Mary: When I returned to Egypt, I was privileged to work closely with Coady staff as the facilitator of one of their overseas projects in Egypt: Transparency, Accountability and Good Governance (TAG). In this project, I experienced a different way of working — it was all about inspiration and influencing change through networks with like-minded people. The project sought to build the capacities of leadership around specific areas of accountability and transparency based on civic values. Each participant designed their own initiative to influence the social change they would like to achieve. The work was done in an innovative way with informal settings for meetings, using new facilitation techniques, fun and play, informal exchange and personal reflection as part of the learning. This approach resulted in a high level of commitment and volunteerism and a lifelong change. It was an eye-opening experience for me on the importance of relationships among different stakeholders and the interaction of individuals within the communities. This experience shaped a different working paradigm for me centred around humans and their relationships.

Both these stories tell us that honest relationships with others are key in any development work. Engaging people and seeking every opportunity for them to be part of a meaningful process, with openness and transparency, are key factors for social change. They can offset any delay in moving ahead and can help sort out any confusion that may occur. We can build relationships with stakeholders for the purpose of project implementation, to overcome certain obstacles such as social and religious stigma, to supplement the lack of resources for media campaigns, or to access certain ethnic groups. We discovered these personal human relationships matter in any transformative work we do with local communities. People's well-being is the ultimate goal of social change. People are the means and the end; they are at the core of all our activities. Social change includes changes in the type of relationship among different actors. Changing the power relationship between different actors and players makes social change real, not a desire. For example, the self-confidence the youth in Kashmir gained, the knowledge and skills they received, made them act differently, and the nature of their relationships with others changed positively.

Acting with Humanity, Ignoring Identity

Mary: What have been some of the memorable moments of your work in such a diverse region of Jammu, Kashmir and Ladakh?

Shaiju: As you know, Kerala is my birth state, the southernmost region of India. As I began this journey of Catholic priesthood, I took the decision to work and live in the State of Jammu and Kashmir (now a Union Territory). Being a Catholic priest in a place where separate regions have Muslim, Hindu or Buddhist majorities, people saw me as an 'outsider' and were suspicious at first. In general, but especially working so closely with the younger generation, I have learned the significance of respecting and learning different traditions and cultures. Simple things such as introducing and encouraging morning prayers to show respect for local religions and culture, and celebrating all festivals such as Eid, Diwali, Holi, Christmas at the training centre was the most natural thing for me. Looking back, during Ramadan months, I also skipped meals with my fasting Muslim colleagues. All this helped develop a healthy and respectful work culture at our training centres.

Mary: I can relate to what you are saying. I used to ask myself about my purpose and identity even before we went to Coady. I had always explored my identity as defined by my social status, professional career, social relationships, and the faith into which I was born. Being at the Coady confirmed and helped reinforce my explorations. With so many people from so many parts of the world I had the privilege to meet, it has been easy to get inspired by individuals from many walks of life, true leaders, who often did not hold formal degrees or senior positions. At Coady, you may remember we were asked to introduce ourselves by our first names only. Weeks later, we discovered each other's jobs and positions! Some of us held high government positions, while others were volunteer activists in their own small communities. This approach enabled us to see the human face first, and not be influenced by official titles and positions, religion, social and professional identities as we connected and related with each other.

It is fascinating for me to hear from you that neither of us looks through exclusive lenses such as religion, sex or social status; we see people as whole human beings. This is also how I want to be treated as human beyond those narrow identities. Despite dominant narratives, we don't seem to see the world around us from a 'minority' lens. We embrace diversity and therefore do not need to be defined or rendered powerless, a victim of a single lens.

This sense of importance of human relationship and respect for others seems to be a thread running through both our work and social lives. In the Diploma Program, our collective experience through debates, discussions, dismantling frames, dominant narratives, the exposures and reassurances that our experiences were valid and important, have all been strong reference points. Our first field trip in August 2011 was to a First Nations powwow. It imprinted an insight and appreciation for the diversity in Canadian society that was otherwise largely known as being white European to the world. Another experience was being part of a co-operative inquiry group to learn about the LGBTQ community. Our choice to explore this community, particularly with you Shaiju as a Catholic priest, wasn't well received by some of our other classmates. A deep dive into this community helped us value and appreciate all human life and develop a humane attitude towards all.

Navigating Different Identities
Mary: How is being a priest helpful or a barrier in your work with youth?

Shaiju: Being a Catholic priest and an outsider has had its advantages and disadvantages. In 2012, the government held an orientation for the Block Development Officers (BDO) of Kashmir. All Project Implementing Agencies were invited to make a presentation. After DB Tech presented, a certain BDO in the group raised a concern as to why a Christian non-government organization (NGO) had been handed the project in Kashmir. He was apprehensive about an NGO entering Kashmir with ulterior motives. I was shocked even though it was not the first time I had heard such concerns. DB Tech was founded in 2008 by the Salesian Fathers (Don Bosco) with the singular focus of providing formal and informal skills to youth to make them employable. One of our staff from Kashmir stood up to the apprehensions of the BDO and explained how the organization had been instrumental in providing skills to thousands of youth across the country. It made me realize how vulnerable we all are with our dominant external identities.

By 2016, DB Tech had trained nearly 15,000 youth and offered employment to at least 70% of them. They worked within the state, and outside as far as 3,000 kms from home in varied job profiles as stewards, front office assistants, customer relationship executives, sales executives, nursing assistants, electricians, etc. Our work got noticed across the DB Tech fraternity due to these successful placements. Our trainees were regularly invited by the government to share their success stories.

While there have been other similar incidents — all due to wrong perceptions about the organization's work and my own — there are memorable experiences where my identity helped facilitate the situation. In 2016, we chanced upon an opportunity to send one trainee from Kashmir to attend an international conference on skills in Sri Lanka. Basharat, a trainee from Srinagar, was chosen to represent the organization. Our placement co-ordinator and I went to see her off at the airport; her mother and two siblings also came along. Srinagar airport is a fortified airport with a huge security deployment. It is easy to mistake the place for a garrison. As per the security protocol, all vehicles and luggage are screened about a kilometre from the terminal, and only passengers and a driver are allowed to pass beyond the gate. We were five people and one passenger. The officer at the gate stopped us and forbade us from going ahead. I began to plead for the family so they would be allowed to go through. The security officer's response shocked me. "You are from the South (outsider), you may go in with the passenger, but not these Kashmiris (locals)," he said. I pleaded with the officer to let us all go in, considering that both he and I are outsiders in Kashmir and in this land to fulfil our duties to the nation. The officer finally relented and let us all go to the terminal.

Shaiju: What about you? How did you navigate your different identities in your community?

Mary: In my work, I wear different hats: a donor hat when I follow up with partners on determining the flow of funds, how they are spent, and ensuring we receive satisfying reports; a capacity building hat when I support partner organizations and communities to acquire new knowledge and skills; and an adult educator hat when I want to provide a safe space for people to reflect on their experience and grow. Some hats or identities may be closer to me than others, but I discovered all of them are useful depending on the situation. Sometimes, playing the role of donor, for example, is empowering for certain groups and enables me to bring some topics to the discussion table.

From our point of view, we know people hold various perspectives about us; they might use gender, religion, position or even our social status to label us. It is important for us to know which hat would be most useful to wear in each situation. The powercube[1] is an inspirational tool we learned at the Coady that helps both of us to understand the spaces, levels and forms of power that exist and how we use our identity to negotiate within them. Our guiding rule is to use our personal power to empower others, to help them and to give voice to the voiceless. Being in the powerful positions that we both sometimes hold is useless if we don't use them to empower others. It is important to understand how others perceive our power, and how we use our power for the public good. Understanding the sources of power is key in all situations.

Being Free in Limiting Structures
Shaiju: How did you manage your time after returning from Coady? Was it easy to fit back into society and immediately apply what you

learned after living in that cocoon-like bubble for five months?

Mary: Not at all! Do you remember during our last session before returning home, we were asked to think about how we would face life back home, what kind of reception we expected from family and colleagues, and to imagine our own expectations and reactions? We were invited in small groups to prepare a role play of our expectations and present it to the plenary. Most of our role plays focused on the challenges we anticipated we'd face at home, mostly in terms of infrastructure. We had enjoyed having internet access, good hygiene, ready-made food, green spaces, no traffic, and all the other good aspects of life in Canada that are not in our countries. Some expected higher positions, higher salaries, and better social status because they successfully completed an international education program. Even with the best expectations about how we would be received at home, we really could not fully imagine or prepare ourselves for all the limiting structures (family, institutions, community) after experiencing a free-spirited learning life, liberation and independence during the five-month program.

During our learning at the Coady, we were constantly told to be responsible for all our decisions, whether personal or educational. We decided our own courses, our voluntary work, how we would benefit from all the resources around us. We also carried the responsibility of being independent and living alone for five months without the support systems we were used to in our respective communities. After learning and growing in many ways, being challenged and shifting our thinking, becoming aware of and reinforcing our value systems, we were then asked to fit back into the same old limiting structures at home, to continue living as mainstream persons do in our societies. But we had changed, often at our core. If you recall, many of us in our cohort decided to become freelance consultants rather than go back to their regular work within institutional boundaries; others moved to different organization for higher positions, some even started their own organizations. Many of us realized our new thinking and aspirations did not align well with our organizations, even though, ironically those very organizations were the ones that sent us to attend the leadership program at Coady! Many of us resigned to pursue new paths.

In my case, I continued with my sponsoring organization until the project ended a few months after my return. I was then privileged to work as a freelance consultant with Coady in one of the most interesting learning projects in my life — TAG. During this three-year project, I proved to myself it is possible to have seriously engaging, participatory, empowering and meaningful work, and be very organized to meet donor expectations (with some negotiation and compromise from both sides). Recently I went back to work full-time with an international donor institution and am trying to apply what I have learned and also provide space for the people I engage with. Creating a liberating space that is open to innovation within organizations that may not be ready to adjust their systems to embrace change is a challenge, and a source of inspiration and reflection at the same time.

Shaiju: I have a similar experience managing a massive project through training centres located at distances that are not easily reachable in a day. I had to recruit staff who would be responsible and who would account for their actions. It also meant I had to train them, empower them, and most importantly, trust them. We had to make a lot of decisions locally so as to respect the dynamics of each location which was diverse in almost all aspects of life. My negotiations with senior management at DB Tech helped me with such decision making. These decisions ranged from setting duty hours for staff at the centres, to choosing training subjects as per requirements. Persuasive negotiation was key to the success of our placements. We noticed transformation in our placements after we managed to identify the right set of opportunities for youth and their employers. From knocking on the doors of employers to get placements, it shifted to employers visiting us for campus recruitment.

Negotiation does not only occur through discussion and verbal communication, but also through real life situations. I act in the way I want to be treated by others. I embrace differences, tolerate mistakes, appreciate others and am open in expressing my thoughts. One way to negotiate the limiting structure of a workplace is to do what you really believe in, even if it is only on a small scale, yet satisfying for yourself. I found myself playing some roles that were not required in my position. I learned how to fill the gaps, not only to be in the front lines, but also to come from behind, making sure there is a backup structure for everybody to succeed. Such small things enabled me to carve out more space from the controlled, limiting work environment where I could influence youth to be active citizens in their communities.

Growth involves Pain and Frustration

Shaiju: It sounds like going back from the Coady was not easy. Is this true?

Mary: Living a transformative experience is not always associated with positive words; sometimes you experience frustration. My experience at the Coady helped me to discover my potential and new abilities and skills I did not know I had. I practiced and lived my potential; I grew and learned a lot. The metaphor that comes to mind is when a butterfly comes out of its cocoon, it is hard for it to go back and shrink into its old, limiting structure. This is also what happened to me when I came back to Egypt. I came back to a limiting community structure, organizational hierarchy and family patriarchy, and found it frustrating. Even now, I feel I have more capacity and a lot to offer, but I have to fit into limiting structures that do not grow with me. At this point, negotiating this complexity is important, as is having the wisdom to let the structure stretch to fit you, and sometimes to wait for others' growth as well. In fact, not only after the Coady, but also after doing my master's degree in the UK, coming back to my community was not easy. Negotiating limited structures after experiencing growth is challenging, but also empowering. I enjoy looking back to all that I have been through and sharing these successes; that pain can be a blessing.

Values for Managing Complexity in Life

When our group coined the slogan "Coady brings us together" for the class T-shirt, little did any of us think it would have such an impact in our lives. It has been a decade since we were together, living with the same group, learning from each other and having life-enriching experiences. Yet, our bond and mutual admiration is strong even today. The experience at the Coady helped us to appreciate life, the differences within it and to provide space for expression.

We firmly believe the pedagogy at the Coady during our time had a transformative effect in our lives as we became more aware of ourselves, our beliefs and our capacity to make positive change, both on a personal level and within the community, despite the limitations of existing structures.

The different stories we shared here represent key milestones in our lives and how we managed to apply our learning in our local communities. Negotiating the complexity of life and work was not easy. It required several trials and calls for perseverance. Reflecting on how we managed this complexity has revealed several values we have in common: sympathy, cultural sensitivity, perseverance, celebrating differences, appreciating the human spirit, challenging structures to effect positive change by using the power within; and above all, the importance of good human relationships.

Endnotes

1   powercube: Understanding power for social change: https://www.powercube.net/analyse-power/what-is-the-powercube/

Dear citizen

If economic security
I mean agency I mean
justice is not bred to
move in political realms
is it because the path is simply
one of snakes and ladders, spirals
because we don't find the right
balance of love and power,
between growing trees and
navigating jungles or we chickegg
the poor thing into parts until
it's stuck or dying
failed to watch
how it moved. Is it
because we miss in it
the moral power, the
imagination, intoxication,
the trust, the critical
intangible of the
townhouse, the gathering,
the dialogue, this dialogue,
our kite and our stars.

nanci lee

This found poem was generated from a forum that I participated
in at the Coady Institute on the links between economic and
political citizenship, June 27, 2014

Unlearning to Change

*Old ways of thinking and acting have been
broken up and a new spirit has gone abroad.*

Rev. James (Father Jimmy) Tompkins
Knowledge for the People, 1921

Seven

Learning to unlearn: Indigenous knowledge systems and spirituality

Alice Ndlovu, Zimbabwe

Sometimes it takes a big change to make a big change! Many years ago, I left an organization I had been working with for seven years, to join Muonde Trust, a small community-based organization in my birth community Mazvihwa, in rural Zimbabwe. I was coming from an organization with strict programming systems to join a group of farmers who were working the best way they knew how. It was a clash of cultures inside me. I made the change because I wanted to experience something new; there was a gap within I always felt after coming back from work. The change of workplace and community was the beginning of a demanding journey for me, full of ups and downs, and lots of learning and unlearning as a development professional. I invite you to journey with me as I reflect on these experiences.

The whole first year with Muonde Trust I spent trying to "formalize" the organization and their work. Looking back now I think formalizing a non-profit organization is overrated. What I did do well was to register the organization officially and put some administrative structures in place. In terms of programming, I was not sure what I was doing. I was in a transition mode trying to learn and understand the farmers' way of doing things, while at the same time assuming a leadership role.

This is the community I grew up in. I had also worked here with another organization with an entirely different set up than I was now facing in Muonde Trust. Many issues came into play that emerged out of my lived experience: from childhood through to my tertiary education level; from implementing projects with a local organization; from being with other community members working in our organization trying to make our lives better. I realized I was still stuck in a programming model where we had to do things in line with funding requirements. Now, I was faced with people who already knew what they wanted, were already doing it, and who were in need of minimal external intervention. Looking back now, I can see a point where I was overbearing and confusing to both myself and to them. I was fortunate to have Dr. Ken Wilson as an advisor to Muonde. He has a wealth of experience working with Indigenous communities including mine. He made, and is still making, my journey interesting and worthy.

The Learning Road to Self Discovery

After working with Muonde for a couple years, I was privileged in 2015 to embark on a real journey which I now call a "learning road to self-discovery." On this journey, my first stop was Baltimore, United States of America to an EDGE conference[1]. This conference brought people together to consider four goals: to decommodify nature, reimagine work, liberate knowledge and democratize wealth. I had an opportunity to co-present with colleagues from Borneo and the Amazon region. This was an eye opening learning experience for me, both to meet like-minded organizations and to know that there are people who support the kind of work my community is doing. On arriving at the conference, I still thought the community had to shift to do things differently: more in line with what other organizations were doing and similar to what I had learned in school. Being at the conference was the first indication for me that this journey was going to mean a lot of self-introspection.

After the EDGE conference I had an opportunity to attend two courses at the Coady International Institute in Canada. One of the courses was *Building on Local and Indigenous Knowledges for Community Resilience (BLIK)*. This course was another eye opener; using practical examples, videos and case studies, it gave me information on Indigenous knowledge systems from around the world. I was also able to learn from people from different countries. Our discussions and sessions resonated with the work I was doing at home! I realized the war I had within myself was about how I could incorporate the knowledge I acquired as a development worker with the work that my community is doing, without losing the Mazvihwa way of life in the process. During the course I was introduced to the endogenous development concept. This was the moment I learned it is possible to work with indigenous knowledges AND appropriate external knowledge. On one of our trips, we met Mi'kmaw Elder Albert Marshall who spoke about the concept of "two eyed seeing"[2] which refers to learning to see from one eye with the strength of indigenous knowledge and ways of knowing, and from the other eye to see the strengths of Western knowledges and ways of knowing, and learning to use both of these eyes for the benefit of all. This was an "aha" moment for me, as it was a wise solution to the equation I was trying to solve in my mind.

Another thing that was activated on this journey was connecting with my spirituality. This was enhanced in the BLIK course by the morning activity we did every day called "mystica." This kind of activity was new to me, coming from a Christian background. In the many workshops I have attended the only way to start a day was to conduct a Christian prayer; for me that was the only activity I thought connected me with my spiritual being. I realized connecting with my spirituality on a journey commenced during the BLIK course because I opened up to learning to respect other people's beliefs. I felt it helped me reach a balance. The mystica opened my mind through diverse and creative activities in the morning that made my learning easier. Without the mystica activities, I would have blocked everything that happened and that would have affected my learning process.

It was during the BLIK course that we interacted with people from the Mi'kmaq First Nation in Canada and had the opportunity to participate in a sweat lodge and powwow. A sweat lodge is a sacred ceremony of cleansing and rejuvenation, and a powwow is a cultural celebration. These are experiences I will treasure for the rest of my life. It taught me how bad it is to demonize other people's beliefs without even allowing yourself to learn or understand them. When I came back from the sweat lodge, I felt liberated. The feeling came from the fact that for the first time I had done something I wanted to, without the fear of being judged. When I came out of the sweat lodge, I was still a Christian. There was nothing done in the sweat lodge that was against what I believed; no one was forced to do anything, all the activities were done willingly. When I got back home, I was a changed person, open minded and I started accepting people as they are. I felt I was no longer a danger to myself and even to the people around me. I no longer lived in the shadow of anyone. If we as human beings do not discover ourselves, we become a danger to ourselves and to people around us.

Interrogating Colonialism

During this period of learning, there are other things I did not grasp well. I remember our session on colonization. I got angry! The discussion raised a lot of debate and emotions, and the part that angered me most was when the role played by missionaries in colonization was discussed. I remember writing a message to Ken Wilson during the break; the message was full of anger and misplaced emotions! I can't remember the message word for word, but I was talking about how bad religion is and how many African cultures were eroded by other cultures. His response was very calming. He responded the journey of working with indigenous knowledge comes with a sense of responsibility and respecting others; we can work on supporting different African cultures without hating other people's beliefs. After we went back into the session, we had a ceremony where we burnt our negative feelings and emotions. It was during this ceremony I discovered how training can be dangerous to a practitioner if personal reflection is not emphasized. Without reflection, personal and with others in this session, I could have travelled back to Zimbabwe sour and sowed the wrong seeds in my community. My lesson here was to understand the subject first and deal with whatever emotions I had inside me, to understand myself, before even talking about the subject and my reactions with my community. It was also important to analyze from my own perspective whether it was a safe subject for discussion.

That particular incident taught me the importance of learning to understand myself before thinking of sharing. We must be able to fill our own cups before sharing. That process of filling one's cup is reflective and can lead to an in-depth understanding of any subject because you can consult, and consider it deeply before taking action. When I went back to my community I started working on my self-noticing and embracing the changes I was seeing in how I was relating to people of different religions and beliefs. I stopped judging people and started developing an interest in different cultures and learning about them. I also discovered the Muonde team was rich in information that was good for the development of our organization. It made my work and my life easier. As human beings, we are spiritual beings. If you go to someone without an open mind or with a judgmental spirit you will not be easily accepted. In our area of work, people need to accept and trust to share with you.

I did not start talking with my community about the issue of colonization until 2016, after a workshop in Ghana. I had come back from Canada in 2015 and started to look for ways to share what I had learned about the effects of colonialism, but could not find a way I felt confident about. Not everyone takes that long to find themselves. For me it was a necessary delay which yielded positive results. I needed to find a balance to deal with all the information and skills I had and discover how I could use them to help my community, without losing myself in the process. The workshop in Ghana, which was also on indigenous knowledges for community resilience, gave me what I needed to achieve this balance. I was able to go to the field and interact with community people from another place besides mine. It also helped that two people from my organization were with me; this gave me confidence.

Making the Learning Practical

Back in Zimbabwe, with the information I had amassed on endogenous development and from my spirituality journey, we started a process of restoring our sacred sites. We got funding to restore the sacred forest called Rambotemwa in Zimbabwe. What made it easier was the practical nature of the BLIK course activities. During the courses in Canada, we used a lot of case studies, written articles and videos. This type of learning brought to life the ideas and lessons we were studying.

The restoration of the Rambotemwa site came with many rituals. Elders wanted to dedicate the forest to the ancestors so as to return sacredness to the forest. It was done amicably. The team started by interviewing community Elders who highlighted what people had done wrong, such as the allocation of homesteads and cutting down trees in the sacred forest. The Elders resolved the only way forward was to appease the ancestors. I was able to give the necessary support and information I had learned in the BLIK course and my experiences with indigenous communities in Ghana. I treasure these experiences and they benefit our community by bringing back our sense of identity. Other neighbouring communities are now inviting us to help with information and planning on how they can restore their sacred sites. The best thing is that now others are involved. The community leaders have been sending messages to their neighbouring communities that they are free and willing to assist them. I am not the only one who can help in restoring their sacred sites.

Respect and Working Together

Respect is another value I nurtured during my experiences at Coady. I feel respect is linked to my spiritual journey and is part of an in-depth understanding of indigenous knowledges. Respect is at the core of development work; it is a word that has a multifaceted meaning. I learned respect is comprised of respecting myself, my beliefs, and also other people's spirituality and different way of doing things. I learned this value during my first week of training at the Coady in 2015. It continues to help me in my day-to-day life and interactions with family, colleagues and community members.

In Mazvihwa and many other African societies there are things we were never taught. We learned through socializing and interacting with others. What may be deemed normal in my community, can be a taboo in another. Considering this was the first time I was in a learning environment with people from different cultures, there was great need for me to embrace the value of respect. There is no way one can be an island during a three-week certificate course or a six month leadership development course with others from around the world. There was every need and desire to make friends. This was only achievable by embracing each other's personal and cultural differences and learning to co-exist peacefully in our learning and living spaces. This helped me to host volunteers and visitors from different countries that come to our community.

Respect does not come easy. It comes with hard work and compromise. Sometimes you can offend someone unknowingly, so journaling, reflection and self-introspection enabled me to see and work on my mistakes. It is a continuous process which requires a lot of dedication and acceptance when you are wrong. In my organization, most people I work with do not have a formal education; they are chosen for their dedication and innovation in the community. Among the team of 26 people, four people have university degrees, and I am the only one with a master's degree and NGO experience. Before learning about respect, I used to believe I knew everything that was required even if I did not publicly show it. I disregarded a lot of suggestions from my colleagues based on principles I learned in school. The concept of "two-eyed seeing" assisted me in understanding and working with both Indigenous knowledges from community members and with Western knowledges that are normally taught in school. Now during our discussions and meetings, we look at all ways of knowing and come to a common understanding that works for everyone. This respect for different ways of knowing has improved our work and our working relationships.

The interactions with the BLIK facilitators, David Fletcher and Bern Guri were also influential. When we worked together co-facilitating two workshops in Ghana and Kenya, the experience taught me how to be a good team member. They saw a little seed in me which they nurtured. I have grown and matured from the first workshop I co-facilitated with them in Ghana to the one we co-facilitated in Kenya. This maturation happened because I was working with people who respected me as an equal. One of the sessions I led in Kenya was on gender and equity in indigenous knowledges. This session was based on my experience, but I had never taught it as an area of learning for people. The way I was treated in these training sessions as a co-facilitator gave me a lot of ideas on how to work with the Muonde team regardless of my privilege of formal education and experience. I learned the importance of accepting people as equally good and that education does not always define a person. Their experiences are of paramount importance to the work we do. If a person is appreciated and honoured, they give their all. That is what I am experiencing now in my organization.

My approach to working with people has changed. My first action when I came back after the Coady Diploma Program in 2017 was to independently give my team responsibilities, allowing them to make mistakes and learn from those mistakes, as a process of self-development. I have seen it helping me grow in the way I was interacting with Bern, David and Ken. I wanted to give my colleagues the same opportunity. I was confident it was going to help my team and would spiral to the community at large. For the first time we sat down together and made a structure which decentralized power in the organization. We managed to promote six people to lead separate teams that work on different programs. This has improved deliverables in our organization and lessened the burden I used to shoulder.

Learning and unlearning is an important process which helps a person become a better version of yourself so that you can live well with others.

Endnotes

1 "EDGE Funders Alliance organizes within philanthropy to raise awareness and deepen understanding of the interconnected nature of the social, economic and ecological crises threatening our common future. EDGE works to increase resources for communities and movements creating systemic change alternatives for a transition to a society that supports justice, equity and the well-being of the planet." EDGE Funders Alliance: https://www.edgefunders.org/

2 "Mi'kmaq Elder Albert Marshall of Eskasoni, Nova Scotia, in the Traditional Territory of Mi'kma'ki, coined the English phrase "Two-Eyed Seeing" many years ago for a guiding principle found in Mi'kmaq Knowledge as reflected in the language. One can see anything or any situation from both a Western scientific viewpoint and a Mi'kmaq Indigenous scientific viewpoint. The recognition and honouring of both viewpoints provides deep insights. Elder Marshall is a fluent speaker of Mi'kmaq ... Two-Eyed Seeing in his language is known as Etuaptmumk."
http://www.integrativescience.ca/uploads/files/Two-Eyed%20Seeing-AMarshall-Thinkers%20Lodge2017(1).pdf

Eight

Personal mastery and systems thinking in Canadian Indigenous communities

Corey Wesley, Anishinabek Nation, Canada

It's late summer on the north shore of Lake Superior. As I cut and cleared the woodland undergrowth and brush at my new camp, I realized the western way of thinking — to clear the competition — is strikingly similar to what I was doing. I was wiping out the smaller trees and shrubs so sunlight could reach directly through. But as I cut brush that in my judgment didn't warrant surviving, suddenly I realized I was cutting into the habitat of insects and burrows of woodland rodents. I had seen coyotes, a bear and bear cub, a fox, a mink, skunks, squirrels, nighthawks, bats, spiders, mice, and much more on this small tract of land. I realized I was encroaching on these invisible habitats — these intricate eco-systems that I could not see. I justified it to myself: they will survive, they will just move on. But later, on the way to my home in the city, I saw the coyote I hadn't seen for a while, dead on the side of the road. She was on the road because she had nowhere else to go. I had chased her off and she died. As I reflected from a systems thinker's point of view, this is a classic example of a tragedy of the commons. Everyone wants a piece of land to themselves, the coyote had nowhere else to go; her habitat had already been encroached upon, and I was the final straw in this entangled and connected system that we both shared.

That late summer of 2017, was also when I prepared to travel to Nova Scotia to attend the Coady International Institute's *Certificate in Learning Organizations and Change.* I went, not knowing exactly what to expect, but I was open to the opportunity for learning new insights, which came fast upon arrival! On what was to be our first day of class, the course instructors changed plans overnight and sent course participants an invitation to participate in a two-day Mother Earth Climate Justice Symposium. We were blessed to hear the late Grandmother and world-renowned water protector, Josephine

Mandamin, give a keynote address on the "Sacredness of Mother Earth and Water." At the time, I did not recognize the unique ability of course instructors to recognize a valuable and relevant learning opportunity, and rapidly adjust to optimize it; but I did know I was in the right place at the right time! As an Anishinaabe[1] man, this initial, immersive and highly inclusive experience, coupled with the rich inter-cultural learning environment of the certificate, where ideas and dialogues about personal mastery and systems thinking were awakened and affirmed, was actually an inherent part of the quality of who we, as Anishinaabe, are.

This essay explores that awakening and suggests how the inherent qualities of Canada's Indigenous Peoples might be awakened and re-affirmed, and serve to advance our fundamental rights whilst contributing to transforming Canada into a just and equitable nation for all Canadians, and perhaps could serve as a model of hope for the world.

Our Past meets Current Learning Organization Theory
Four hundred years ago, my Anishinaabe ancestors were an integral part of the river and watershed system situated between the world's grandest lake, known then as Gitchee-Gaming, now known as Lake Superior, and Hudson Bay, a continental sea of the Artic Ocean. Every day my ancestors followed a discipline of personal mastery. They were continually clarifying and deepening their personal vision, focusing their energies and setting a realistic view of the world around them. They were not only surviving, but thriving. Their interest was not in an individualistic form of growth and development, but rather a calling to a higher purpose, a sense of helping those around them with the vision of a better future. Because they inhabited a very natural and undisturbed ecosystem in the Boreal Forest — the world's largest forest circling the northern hemisphere — their mindset was formed by nature. Their thriving was based on their inherent understanding and being as one with nature — they were holistic systems thinkers. My ancestors were masters in understanding the interconnectedness of everything. Every day, they thought in systems.

Until one day, the holism and interconnectedness they so honoured was catastrophically disrupted. Foreign invaders brought war to our territory; we fought valiantly, but many died. Then came deadly diseases such as smallpox, yellow fever, typhus, and the plague, killing the people and weakening their clan systems. As more and more invaders came, the ecosystem collapsed, and starvation set in. This invasion was followed by the suppression of our culture, assimilation, acculturation, and relocations to human reservations and residential schools. Because of this, the Anishinaabe people became lost in a system that was foreign to our way of thinking, and our worldviews were deeply altered forever.

Today, the impacts from these historical and multi-generational traumas are visible in the descendants of these ancestors, who bear the brunt of the effects from this cataclysmic shift in ways of thinking. Today, we experience marginalization; direct, structural, and systemic racism; violence; and disparities in health and socio-economic status. Many to this day live in despair and feel they have no place on this Earth.

As a descendant of this timeline, I too have experienced the impacts of historic and multi-generational trauma. I have struggled, but I overcame. I have been down, but I climbed my way back up. Along the way, I was blessed to be introduced to mentors and elders that have taught me the disciplines of personal mastery and systems thinking. Because of this, I decided to make it my mission to heal my own trauma, be the best version of myself that I could be, so I could help others. At one point, I didn't know if I would live to see my 24th birthday. But now, I hold a Master of Science in Kinesiology, I have four children, and I am an award-winning entrepreneur in the fitness industry as a strength and conditioning coach for aspiring and pro hockey players.

On the path to healing my own trauma, I have come to understand the ancestral wisdom of the Anishinaabe people, who hold stories of personal mastery and systems thinking; and through these stories, a life can change and the world around you, as you perceive it, can change. I will share some of my own experiences in working with traditional knowledge and the current theory of learning organizations.[2] The different knowledge systems are complementary and much can be learned from each of them, and hopefully from dialogue between them.

When I talk about systems thinking with others, the first question that comes up is: What is systems thinking? My response is: Ok, well asking questions means you are on the right track to becoming a systems thinker.

How I Explain Systems Thinking

"We live in a dense and tangled global system in which everyone has a different vantage point. No one person can explain what is going on to everyone else or assume that his or her point of view is the right one."[3]

I know of two types of systems thinking, one is linear and the other is circular.

Linear systems thinking is concerned with understanding the parts of a system, in order to understand the whole. However, dissecting the parts of a system to understand how to make changes to the whole has its issues. Separating, dissecting, and zooming into 1% of a system causes you to lose sight of the rest — the other 99% of the system. This process is very reductionist and is a common mental model in the Western worldview.

Another worldview used to solve everyday problems in our communities, requires you become a circular systems thinker. Circular systems thinking examines systems holistically, and focuses on building ideas versus separating and dissecting parts. It examines the relationship of a system's parts and uses ideas, generated from dialogue with others, who have a different vantage point in the system, to discover positive changes that can be put into action.

For example, consider two scenarios concerning the same child with two different teachers:

In the first classroom, the teacher is a linear thinker and is concerned one of her students may have attention deficit hyperactivity disorder (ADHD), and refers the child to a specialist to diagnose and possibly prescribe medication so the child will stop interrupting her class.

In the second classroom, another teacher who thinks more circularly is also concerned for the same child however, she does not assume he has ADHD. She is aware the child travels from the Indian reserve and is the only Indigenous student in the class. She speaks with the child's mother, and finds out the child's favourite cousin committed suicide two months earlier. He now spends most of his time locked in his room, where he has developed an addiction to his smart phone. Looking at the situation holistically, this teacher realizes the child is suffering emotional grief and his addiction to his smart phone is affecting both his mental and physical health. Through dialogue with his mother and the school board, they put a holistic plan in place, referring the child to a traditional Indigenous healer in the community, who addresses the emotional, physical, mental and spiritual aspects of the young student, and help him on a personal healing journey.

In a linear thinking mental model, the child would have been referred to a Western trained doctor, who would have diagnosed the child's symptoms as being a disruptive student in class. By contrast, in the circular, holistic mental model, the child's trauma, which is the root cause of the disruptive behaviours, is addressed and the student begins action on a healing journey that will have positive ramifications for all those he surrounds himself with in the present and the future. In a system, all elements are interconnected.

Interconnectedness[4] is Fundamental to Circular Systems Thinking

Systems thinking involves a shift in our individual and collective mindsets, one where we move away from the linear ways of thinking that have been engrained into us from Western worldviews to that of a circular mindset. In the linear mental model, A impacts B, therefore C is impacted. For example, as an Indigenous person, thinking circularly comes naturally to me and is embedded in my culture. The fundamental principle of this shift is that everything is interconnected. From a health perspective, health is not just how healthy you are physically. Health is a balance of physical, emotional, mental and spiritual health. If one aspect is unbalanced, the other three will be affected.

Essentially, we understand everything is reliant upon something else for survival. Humans need food, air, and water to sustain our bodies, and trees need carbon dioxide and sunlight to thrive. Everything needs something else, often a complex array of other things, to survive.

Inanimate objects are also reliant on other things: a chair needs a tree to grow to provide its wood, and a cell phone needs electricity distribution to power it. So, when we say "everything is interconnected" from a systems thinking perspective, we are defining a fundamental principle of life. From this, we can shift the way we see the world, from a linear, structured mechanical worldview to a dynamic, chaotic, interconnected array of relationships and feedback loops.

Systems thinkers use this mindset to untangle and work within the complexity of life on earth. They ground both their thinking and subsequent action on the principle of interconnectedness and circular thinking.

Mental Models and the Indigenous Worldview

In order to be allowed to vote in Canada, you have to be "human." Indigenous people in Canada were not allowed to vote prior to 1960 because the colonial system labeled Indigenous people as "non-humans." Indigenous people argued that we are, in fact, human beings, and this obvious systemic barrier was unacceptable. A movement was led against this systemic inequity.

Colonial thinking of the time was a way to constrict Indigenous Peoples. Only a select few 'elite' held the key to legislative and economic power. These select few considered their theories to hold the highest priority. As a result, this colonial philosophy was subjugated into Indigenous Peoples and dominated as the main narrative of their mental model. History was rewritten and Indigenous People's history faded from the history books. Thus the 'Story of History' is looked at with great skepticism by both Indigenous people and systems thinkers. Historical truth is hidden within the narrative point of view advocated by the dominant culture.[5]

Our patterns of thinking and our behaviours are shaped by our mental model. Personal Mastery is about shaping our mental models to control the factors that we can, so that when there are unintended consequences, or fixes that fail in the system, we can adapt and be resilient in how we overcome those consequences. My ancestors valued a mental model of personal mastery, because they were interdependent on each other as a community, and with the environment and ecosystem that surrounded them and in which they were a profound part. Four hundred years ago if there was a change in the ecosystem, one of two things happened in the Canadian North. You died, or you survived. Learning how to survive meant that you could thrive while you were alive. The system enacted a pattern of interdependency that shaped our patterns of thinking and our actions. Over time, with the introduction of other disruptive worldviews, the system changed and so did our knowledge and practice of interdependency.

Mental models are the values that you hold, your assumptions, biases, educational background, and your lived experiences that have shaped how you look at the world. Colonization deeply shifted how Indigenous people understand the world around them. Cultural revitalization is important not only for Indigenous people, but for all of us who benefit from the self-revitalizing environment and ecosystem. In order to revive our old traditions that are in line with the interconnectedness with the natural world, we must hold on to the knowledge of the Elders, who have had a set of experiences that compels us to think and see the world differently.

When I was a child, we used to drive to the community my grandmother lived in, deep in the boreal forest in Northwestern Ontario, Canada. The highway drive was lined with beautiful jack pine, poplar, birch and cedar trees; it gave us a sense that our ecosystem was healthy. Then one day, I had a chance to go for a helicopter ride over the territory. I could see the entire landscape, and as far as the eye could see onto the horizon. It was a lifeless clearcut of the forest! The only places that had trees were along the highways and roadways. At that point I realized the land was not healthy. I felt I had been lied to because the forest seemed so healthy when driving along the highway corridor. The linear mental models held by industry focus on individuality and profits and have resulted in unsustainable practices that have left the Earth's landscape scarred worldwide.

Faced with this destruction, I decided to shift my worldview to one where intergenerational responsibility was at the core. I felt I must take seriously the necessity that the well-being of future generations is largely dependent upon the choices and decisions I make today and during my lifetime. My grandmother then shared with me that the choices we make today will not only affect our children, but seven generations from now. It is said it will take seven generations to heal from the mass destruction that Indigenous people have faced from the destruction of their land and the devastation of their culture. My generation has been called the Seventh Generation from the time colonization started to deeply impact our people. This Seventh Generation mental model gives me hope for the future. However, it will take a long time to heal from the degradation that has been caused to the Earth. The climate will change, global temperatures will rise and we will see more frequent extreme weather events. However, it will take a major paradigm shift to help the world understand that what we do affects not only other parts of the system today, but other parts of the system for future generations. Indigenous people have taken it into their own hands to be stewards of the Earth. In the linear mental model, there are winners and there are losers, but in the long run we will all be losers. It is time to shift our mental models to a model of intergenerational responsibility, adapt and change the way we look at the Earth, and do what we can today to help the future generations and the ecosystems of tomorrow.

Anishinaabe ancestral wisdom — inclusive of mental models of intergenerational responsibility, a deep recognition of interconnectedness, and an honouring of circular systems thinking — is a holistic worldview and knowledge system that has been marginalized for generations. A revival of that wisdom tradition can contribute much to changes needed in the world today and the strengthening of all communities and groups that strive to be learning organizations.

Endnotes

1 Anishinaabe (other variants include Anishinabe, Anicinape, Nishnaabe, Neshnabé and Anishinabek) refers to a group of culturally and linguistically related First Nations that live in both Canada and the United States, concentrated around the Great Lakes. https://www.thecanadianencyclopedia.ca/en/article/anishinaabe

2 Senge, P. (1990). The Fifth Discipline: The art and practice of learning organizations. New York, NY: Doubleday/Currency.

3 Wheatley, M. (2000). Cultivating uncertainty in a complex world. The Systems Thinker, Vol.10, no. 9. para. 4. https://thesystemsthinker.com/wp-content/uploads/pdfs/110905pk.pdf

4 Acaroglu, L. (2017). Tools for Systems Thinkers: The 6 fundamental concepts of systems thinking. https://medium.com/disruptive-design/tools-for-systems-thinkers-the-6-fundamental-concepts-of-systems-thinking-379cdac3dc6aa

5 Toscano, A. (2008). The open secret of real abstraction. Rethinking Marxism, Vol. 20, no. 2, pp. 273-287.

— Nine —

Questioning the dominant ableist narrative in social justice education

Pamela Johnson, Canada

"This may feel true for every era, but I believe I am living in a time where disabled people are more visible than ever before. And yet while representation is exciting and important, it is not enough. I want and expect more. We all should expect more. We all deserve more."

Alice Wong[1]

When I learned I would be joining the team at the Coady International Institute, it felt like an alignment of many things. For me, it represented a space that exemplified a unique and ideal blending of the study of development born out of citizen-led, community-driven change, and an opportunity to be surrounded with people and perspectives from around the globe. Within my role at the institute, I had the opportunity to come together with participants, facilitate a space where they would share their knowledge and experiences, dig into collaborative analysis and push our collective understanding from the purview of life experiences of people from around the world.

Where it Started for Me

I have worked and volunteered alongside people with disabilities for the majority of my adult life, and have had the privilege of being mentored by many strong advocates and educators. Much of the collaborative work we engaged in together was rooted in advocacy that is related to gaining greater access and accommodation within large institutions or systems — schools, healthcare and/or housing. Early in my time at the Institute, I showed an interest in how participants with disabilities were accessing courses and scholarships within our programs. After several months, participants with disabilities began approaching me to talk about their various experiences at the

Institute. I often heard stories relating immense struggles in initially getting to the Institute. Not unlike most international participants, they had to overcome barriers such as dealing with visas, permission to leave work, and family. However, participants with disabilities had their worry compounded by additional barriers concerning how they would maneuver their physical and learning accommodations on campus and in the classroom.

Some identified thoughtful aspects of access and planning on campus such as elevators and ramps, as well as a lack of access that felt 'othering.' The doors on the beautiful and newly renovated library were large and heavy and did not have accessible features. Anyone who could not open the door had to catch the attention of the staff inside. Some participants also spoke about the social exclusion they felt in being housed away from their peers, so as to meet their own needs for an accessible dorm room. They spoke of their difficulty in the lack of looping (a special type of sound system for use by people with hearing aids) in classrooms for participants who required FM systems, and the lack of accommodations for people who are visually impaired and without a guide. This inaccessibility is at the root of exclusion — if you cannot get into the building, how can you contribute to the conversation?

Beyond the conversations with participants, I also heard from a prominent leader in the disability community in Canada who informed me at a conference that they would never recommend any woman with a disability to take courses at our Institute due to the multiple concerns raised with her about a lack of access and representation. Thinking about the graduate who had spoken to this leader, I felt badly for the graduate, and was embarrassed for our institution. I promised to do something to address the concerns they listed.

Putting Access and Accommodation on the Agenda

These stories were not unfamiliar to me. I have heard and witnessed persons with disabilities and their families come up against systemic ableism and subsequent challenges to access education, suitable and decent housing and gainful employment. As a dear friend says, "People with disabilities are the ultimate life hackers!" Persons with disabilities learn early on that most of the accommodations they require to fully participate will need to be made

by and for themselves, as universal design is too often led by
non-disabled people.

So, when we know the majority of the people designing our educational spaces and writing our educational content are not people living with disabilities, how do we ensure that spaces are universally designed and our content reflects the lived experiences of people living with disabilities? Legislation such as the Nova Scotia Accessibility Act and the Accessibility for Ontarians with Disabilities Act help address aspects of access and accommodation for persons with disabilities, but take decades to roll out enforceable regulations. They cannot be relied upon to address deep seated ableism that is pervasive in our country and its institutions.

Famed writer Arundhati Roy said, "The trouble is that once you see it, you can't unsee it. And once you've seen it, keeping quiet, saying nothing, becomes as political an act as speaking out. There's no innocence. Either way, you're accountable."[2] When the participants learned I was not only interested in their stories, but committed to bring some of their concerns forward, they gave me an opportunity to earn their trust and that meant a lot to me.

Seeking Opportunities

As a non-disabled person, I would often bring the topic of access and accommodation to the table at staff and team meetings. I was not the only person who voiced an interest in improving access, and in seeing a growing number of persons with disabilities admitted into our educational programs. I sought out colleagues with similar values who knew we had a duty to do more to actively work towards developing this learning space into one where all students could congregate and learn from one another.

As staff of the Institute, we were invited to submit project proposals that focused on various innovations in teaching and community-based projects. If chosen by the internal review committee, these projects could be funded to develop those 'innovative' ideas. Following two and a half years of discussing (and attempts to convince leadership in the organization) why teaching and learning that included the perspectives, history and social movements of persons with disabilities was critical to our work, we were finally able to secure some funding that permitted our project proposal to move forward. To read more about our collaborative work, see Applying an Intersectional Approach to Facilitating and Global Development Practice.[3]

Barriers to Innovation in Social Justice Learning

While building an argument and rationale for equity I was informed by a colleague that another, former colleague with a disability had submitted an almost identical proposal for interventions a few years prior to my joining the Institute. We had both proposed:

- the development of an affirmative action plan to admit participants with disabilities,
- the development of classroom content detailing the his/herstory of persons with disabilities, their continued civil rights movement, and their leadership in those and other movements, and
- developing an opportunity for co-learning, as not all educators believe they are equipped to share the aforementioned content, nor have they accessed that type of education themselves.

Through this experience, I have identified some of the barriers to innovation, and actions that support the exclusion of marginalized people in a social justice learning institution. As well, I believe I have gained an understanding of how to leverage change in the company of others.

Idolizing institutions and the people within is part of the problem: I do not use the word idolizing lightly. There can be a kind of unwavering faith or absence of questioning that happens in spaces where we feel we ideologically fit. There may even be an assumption that power will not be perverted or misused, especially in a social justice learning organization. I believe many of us know that in spaces where we do not believe we can question or challenge power, you will find injustice and it will be experienced most acutely by those who are already marginalized. When we work and study within these spaces, we have an opportunity and a duty to question who is not included, who is not making decisions, and whose stories we choose not to tell.

The importance of finding allies: When we witness injustice and inequality do we seek to become an ally, or decide to not become involved? Do we advocate for change or stay silent? Advocating for the inclusion of people living with disabilities seems like it should be everyone's business for a number of reasons: it promotes fairness, brings diverse perspectives, and attracts more people to tackle complex issues and share wisdom. Today over a billion people on the planet are living with a disability. We ALL know, love and respect someone who is living with disabilities or we are a person with disability. So, why was it that a colleague with lived experience shared her well researched and supported recommendations for four years and got little reception from the leadership of the organization? Why did it take me, a non-disabled woman, two and a half years to convince them to allow us to take action?

At times when I have felt frustrated because my advocacy is disregarded or ignored, I know I am not alone. I know there are people who are beyond tired, frustrated and angry that their fundamental human rights are ignored, overlooked and not enforced. In that light, my personal frustrations quickly diminish. For anyone reading this who has done any kind of advocacy work, you likely know how lonely that work can be, especially if you have not found 'your people.' We often look to our peers to confirm our understanding of the world. Starting an initiative can be exciting and tremendously motivating, and equally de-motivating and frustrating if others do not see the need for change. Often it is linked to an inability to relate, or a belief that it is not a priority. This may denote a tremendous privilege that is unquestioned even in spaces where the focus of learning is equity and disrupting oppressive, top-down processes. Find your people; you need them and they need you.

Lived experience and expertise is non-negotiable: Convincing leadership that the content for this project needed to be developed in partnership with disabled educators who are experts in global development and adult education can be a barrier. As non-disabled educators, we can continue to amplify the voices of our disabled colleagues, support their work and draw attention to their accomplishments. We need to ask, who has not been included in the conversation? How have students with disabilities been consulted about their experience? Do we have questions in our surveys about access and accommodation?

As non-disabled educators, we can question our role in telling or interpreting the stories of persons with disabilities when they are underrepresented, underpaid and most often, not invited to tell their stories in the classroom. As non-disabled educators, we have an opportunity to insist that we get our content and teaching from experts with that lived experience. The more we hear from and learn from our colleagues, the more competent we will be and feel in promoting their stories, struggles and successes in places of learning, and we will know who to invite to those spaces to share essential teaching. Furthermore, we can ask why experts with lived experience are not in teaching positions, and ensure that when positions are posted we share them with a diversity of peers.

So What?

Efforts were made at the Institute to address the need for increased accessibility: a button was installed on the library door, and attempts to keep students together in the dormitory were employed wherever possible. Several colleagues participated in the co-learning sessions gaining foundational knowledge about universal design for learning, and how to apply the content focusing on persons with disabilities' stories in their courses. There's always more work to do, and a growing number of colleagues appeared interested and ready to learn and rebuild spaces that welcome a more diverse group of participants. I believe the discussions, drawing attention to the importance of the issue, modeling an openness to learning, as well as a persistence and commitment to listen to, respect and follow the recommendations of persons with disabilities, had an impact on us all.

As learners, educators and citizens, we have an opportunity to seek initiatives that include the lived experiences, histories, and accomplishments of all people. We can examine, question and celebrate what is being done in our organizations, local school boards, colleges, universities and social justice institutes. We can support progressive initiatives by amplifying their message and engaging in our own learning and relearning. This experience had a transformative impact on me personally and professionally. I am dogged in my determination for increased access and accommodation and am deferential to my colleagues with lived experience in our mutual work. Finally, I am pleased when I get into 'trouble' with people who are truly disrupting, dismantling and rebuilding spaces that need remediation — this is where my true social justice learning happens.

Endnotes

1 Wong, A. (Ed.) (2020). Disability Visibility: First-person stories from the twenty-first century. New York, NY: Vintage Books, p. xxi.

2 Roy, A. (2001). Power Politics. Cambridge, MA: South End Press 2001, p. 7.

https://thirdworldtraveler.com/Arundhati_Roy/Power_Politics.html

3 Johnson, P., Kraglund-Gauthier, W., & Houston, B. (2018). Applying an Intersectional Approach to Facilitating and Global Development Practice. Antigonish, NS: Coady International Institute, Innovation Series, No.11.
https://coady.stfx.ca/wp-content/uploads/2019/01/IS11.pdf

Johnson, P., Houston, B., & Kraglund-Gauthier, W. (2019). Decolonizing the classroom in social justice learning: Perspectives on access and inclusion for participants living with disabilities. Innovations in Higher Education Teaching and Learning, Vol. 16, pp. 83-95.
https://doi.org/10.1108/S2055-364120190000016009

Ten

Viewing allegiance and accountability in organizations

Balakrishna Venkatesh, India

It has been my good fortune to be working in the development sector after spending the first part of my career in academia and then in the corporate sector. With this background, in 1989 I became passionate about founding an organization managed by Indians with disabilities, which would have at its core the values of self-determination, self-advocacy and inclusion. This indeed happened and I became a founding member of its Board.

Eight years later, I left the organization and began offering my services as a consultant and trainer on disability rights, development and organizational development. In this capacity, I was involved in interventions for many organizations in more than 30 countries. One such intervention was with Save the Children Fund, UK in Ethiopia. The focus of the consultation was on increasing the representation of persons with disabilities in remote communities by working with their innate desire to come together to form self-help groups. During this time, I met Debbie Castle and a new aspect of my career opened up.

In 2005, Debbie invited me to co-design and co-facilitate a new certificate course *Learning Organizations and Change* (LOC) to be offered as a three-week certificate at the Coady International Institute. I asked "Why me?" She replied that my years of experience in setting up self-help groups with persons with disabilities in rural India and the many successes and challenges of working as a consultant would be valuable in conversations with participants about learning and change in organizations and communities.

Once in Canada, we developed the LOC certificate course. We learned so much about organizations in the 10 years we facilitated together, from the resources we accessed, to the reflections on our own lived experiences in organizations, and to the richness brought by the development leaders who participated in the course — more than 200 from as many as 20 countries from the global South.

These annual LOC facilitation experiences led me to reconsider some of the issues faced by organizations, especially those set up by and for persons with disabilities. One of the difficult issues faced by these organizations has at its root, challenging experiences regarding allegiance to a person versus accountability to the people the organization is established to serve. In this essay, stories of three different organizations are shared, some set up specifically by and for persons with disabilities, and others where specific programs for persons with disabilities have been set-up within larger development programs. All the stories relate to attempts made to resolve conflicts caused by ongoing confusion. I can now see these mix-ups can be associated with issues of allegiance and accountability. The stories show about how these conflicts are playing out and about the interventions being introduced in attempts to maintain organizational relevance.

Organization #1

This organization was set up more than 30 years ago as a resource centre to promote and equip existing NGOs in rural India to work with persons with disabilities. The intention was to encourage persons with disabilities to come together to form their own organizations for self-determination and self-advocacy. This aim was, and still is, a very different way of working than found in most NGO work, where the old charity model and doing 'for' persons with disabilities is still being used.

I was the founding Director of this organization for many years. Upon leaving, I was succeeded by a Director who was there for more than eight years, until a new person came on as Chair of the Board of Directors. Acting without the approval of the rest of the Board, this new Chair presented the Director with a dismissal notice. The Chair had someone else in mind to hire as Director. The Director accepted this letter of dismissal and left extremely angry, yet said nothing to the rest of the Board to challenge it. This could be interpreted as a show of allegiance to one's self, to maintain some level of respect and pride, rather than thinking about the persons with disabilities that the organization served and one's accountability to them in the role of Director. Refusing to accept the letter of dismissal would have demonstrated accountability to the people being served rather than allegiance to one's self.

The story gets complicated but that newly hired Director was dismissed within three months of appointment! During this time the organization struggled to serve in the way it had been set up to, and I was invited back to resume the role of Chair of the Board to help revive the organization. In accepting, I made it clear I would invite the previous Director, who had succeeded me years ago, to join the Board as well. That person nominated someone they knew to apply for the Director's position. To avoid any conflict of interest, the other Board members did the interview and did the official hiring. The new person came with a high level of integrity but, as we soon found out, did not have the competencies necessary for the position. The Board agreed to work with this Director to build the necessary competencies using a mentoring process guided by two Board members. Several years have passed and we find this Director is still not able to perform as required in the role.

One analysis of the situation the organization was facing is that the Director has allegiance to the Board member who as a friend told them about the job. There is no accountability to the persons with disabilities for whom the organization exists. This was extremely detrimental to the organization because the person's incompetence was being shielded from the Board by one of its members, making it difficult to introduce changes to programming that required a different set of leadership skills.

An intervention was introduced aimed to ensure the Director understood what accountability meant to the organization. A 360-degree appraisal was set up as part of a revised performance appraisal system. This 360 review was conducted and specific areas for performance improvement for the Director were identified related to program delivery. This process is now in progress and is intended to build accountability to the persons with disabilities served by the organization.

Organization #2:
This story is about another implementing organization that works with persons with disabilities and is committed to using a community-based approach. During the first nine years of this program more than 8,000 persons with disabilities became involved in solving their own problems and creating their own futures. Using such an approach

was not common in the region. After the formative years, an Executive Director was hired who was not accustomed to using community engagement and ownership, and was not very well supervised to do so by the organization. Due to this, the community-based organizations of persons with disabilities (OPDs)started to become dysfunctional. Making sure the members in these OPDs were being nurtured and supported became an important factor in their renewal.

To revive the work in the communities, an intervention was planned to bring the people connected with this organization that were located in the same geographic program areas together. About 60 women and men with different disabilities, with different experiences of the organization over the nine years, came together for two days of interaction, to consider whether the work of this organization could be revived.

During the two days, they experienced the value of being together and their unequivocal desire was to revive the work. As part of the intervention the question was asked, "Who should do this work?" This conversation led to people saying that they wanted to do the work. They also expressed the commitment that even if the organization packed up and left, they would still want to revive the community-based work it had been doing. They said what matters is that we live in these villages and we want the change so we will take responsibility for the work that needs to be done. The conversation then went to how they would do the work on their own accord. They decided to form groups of 12-15 people in each of the different villages to operate as their own organization in a particular geographic area. As an organization they would ask for support from the original implementing organization. They went ahead and asked the organization if it would act as a resource agency to them, helping build their capacity, providing financial resources and handholding as they were taking on 'new-to-them' responsibilities. The organization agreed.

Looking back on this scenario, my analysis is the original implementing organization had lost its way. They had been doing good work with more than 8000 persons with disabilities in their geographic area, but the Executive Committee had become accountable to the donors, rather than to the organization and the persons with disabilities that it serves. When we brought the people who had been receiving the social services together, their allegiance was to people who were living under similar conditions, and they wanted to be accountable for improving conditions with them.

The intervention brought about a shift in governance, where about 60 persons with disabilities are now reclaiming the services, becoming responsible for them and forming small implementing organizations in their villages, called blocks. They can receive funding, support and handholding from the original implementing organization. It's very manageable. Right now, it is stalled because of the COVID-19 pandemic, but the hope is the blocks will soon be active and making a difference in the lives of persons with disabilities in their villages.

Organization #3:
The third scenario helpful in understanding the confusion caused by allegiance and accountability is about an organization that runs an integrated rural development program. It works with desperately poor women and men who belong to the lowest castes in rural areas. It's a huge organization and they also work with persons with disabilities. One of the fundamental principles of their work is forming community-based organizations as self-help groups. By encouraging both these groups of people to form their own groups, the organizations of persons with disabilities (OPDs) have people who are blind speaking with people who are physically disabled, and with parents and family members of children with intellectual disability and cerebral palsy, and talking with people with profound and severe spinal cord injuries and multiple disabilities. It is known that people who are severely or profoundly disabled or have multiple disabilities form a very small percentage of persons with disabilities around the world. In India, this group of persons with severe or multiple disabilities becomes practically invisible, and they are left with no care or support other than what their family can provide.

The intervention in this story was set up to have the OPDs think about this group that was quite invisible to them, and for whom no one but family members were expected to support. What was the OPD's responsibility to persons who were profoundly disabled, as members of their communities? The dialogue about this went on for a year; really, it's still going on, but the intervention has yielded some benefits even if we are still just talking about it. It is a work in progress, but because we started by asking the question of who is responsible, 20% of the self-help groups are taking responsibility to visit the families who have family members who are profoundly and multiply disabled. Children and adults in the families are beginning to give better care, providing showers more often, changing clothes more frequently, and interacting more meaningfully, providing the right food and taking them for health treatments when necessary. For persons with disabilities who are sitting at home and totally dependent on other family members, these changes are creating a better quality of life. Also, the OPDs are managing to give some relief to family members and providing some of this care for the person with profound or multiple disabilities.

In this example we see a shift from being only accountable to the members of your OPD, to also being accountable to those who cannot come to meetings because they are severely disabled, or they are caring for someone who is. Although the work in self-help groups has been going on for more than 30 years, providing care and being responsible for those who are more vulnerable than themselves has been an intervention only in the past three to four years. We are making some progress.

Nurturing Accountability

In the three organizational scenarios described above, positive results have emerged with the focus shifting to being accountable to the people in community, rather than allegiance to one person with whom there is some personal connection. In the first story, the Director may recognize through the 360 feedback they don't have the qualities for the position and leave; or given constructive feedback, they may blossom in new areas. In the second, many of the 8-10 block organizations are implementing what is needed by the people they serve. In the last story, more people involved in the OPDs are finding ways to support the most vulnerable persons with disabilities in their communities and families. In these three scenarios, it is important for people to think about the interventions not as controlling, but rather freeing energy and being an observer; to be there to hold, to comfort, to provide succour, and not to solve problems, but to keep an open mind and make sure accountability is present and intentions are good.

Accountability requires that we become more open-minded and humbler about what is possible and who we are accountable to, that we listen to people, believe they know what they want, and can find the strength to do what they want, and to that extent, take action. So, listening deeply, making sense of what people are saying in a caring environment created with trust, love, and confidence means being accountable to ourselves and to persons with disabilities and OPDs in our communities.

The skills required for this are being able to listen, to challenge in a non-threatening way, pushing people beyond their boundaries of comfort without making them feel small, and having them know if they fail, we are there to catch them.

Other important attitudes for building accountability are being respectful and observing how people interact with each other and what their relationships are like, and who is willing to take responsibility for what they do. Observing the chemistry among people who are present — who is most committed and who might try to break things up due to a lack of interest in self-help groups. Knowing how to build a supportive and nurturing environment, thinking systemically with the people present, and not finding problems in what is happening, but rather seeing everything as a life-giving opportunity to grow from whatever intervention gets planned. Ultimately, the people for whom the intervention is planned should leave feeling good about themselves.

Finally, one thing that has been helpful in this work is having absolute faith in human resilience and capacity, and an insatiable hunger for compassion. The capacity to share and love exists in every human being, and it's a process of tapping into those wellsprings in these interventions; it's not about technique. You can learn this process if you have a mindset that wants to learn and unlearn; often learning is on the other side of unlearning. For any intervention planned, we want something good to come out of it, while allowing the process to play itself out. Each intervention will have its own life with its own spirit, beauty, ugliness and so on that will lead to something positive.

Eleven

Finding a road that was always here

Daren Okafo, Canada

It's 2017 and I'm sitting in my new office at the National Adult Literacy Agency (NALA) in Dublin, Ireland, the city of my birth and my first home. I'm in wonder at this recent return trip — a journey back to this beautiful, terrifying and ancient land of warrior goddesses, old magic and Atlantic mists, of sad songs and sadder struggles, this bloodied and hard-won republic. I had just departed my more recent home in the land of The People, the land of the L'Nu'k, Mi'kma'ki — part of which is now known as Nova Scotia. This return to Dublin is more than physical — it's a journey into transformation, inner and outer. Such journeys of change tend to exist in our lives as threads in an emergent, woven fabric of lived experience — they are infused with emotion, opportunity, regrets and hesitant hopes. They are knit and stitched into a tapestry that speaks of fuller, more connected lived realities, each panel extending and terminating its neighbours, adding context and continuance, constraining what is possible and bridging to what is next, what might come. Just as fabric is more than tangled thread, our tapestries of story are woven and joined, one end leading to other beginnings, branching and interconnected. Occasionally we get to assemble larger panels into another bolt of this emergent fabric of life. We get to witness larger stories unfolding, ones that ripple, recolour and recontextualize everything they touch — like a drop of spilled dye on raw linen.

For me, this journey home was one such moment. Terrifying and bright as a star, bursting with transformative energy, a journey that started in the deepest sadness, leaving my home in Nova Scotia, returning me to Dublin, returning me to the divine loom of my first life, ready to stitch new and old pieces together into cloth that speaks of community and learning, of sharing and of co-creating newness.

This loom metaphor and process of journeying is also a central motif in radical and liberatory adult education and for good reason; the notion of dynamic change is key to transformative learning. Radical pedagogies can be linear and progressive, sequential and causal — we'll move from here to there, taking with us the things we've learned and acquired, while integrating newness and (re)building structures to support change and personal transformation. Like a well-earned journey, they can be cathartic — wonderfully terrifying and challenging, inspiring and productive, overwhelming and existential — but they can also shift, pivot and alter our modes of knowing in more complex, more unexpected ways. They can be non-linear, revealing glimpses and intuitions of new avenues of critique and modes of knowledge construction that may remain inaccessible for now, just over the horizon, hinting at things beyond what we can see clearly, prompting us to begin the construction of a bridge to some unknown but anticipated destination.

As radical educators, we like to talk of transformative pedagogies, as if somehow all learning is not subtly changing us all at all times. It works on us in our quiet moments, long removed from our facilitation efforts in the classroom. It wakes us from our sleep, scrambling for a pen to scribble some poorly considered platitude. We are in a constant state of (be)coming and departing — leaving behind who we once were, and wandering, occasionally with purpose, toward some far-off sign that advertises a person we may yet become. We are all always learning — the more pointed question we pose as radical adult educators is how best can we join this process of becoming so that we can leverage our truest, most authentic and most compassionate practice, welcoming journeys into change as we would a dear friend.

In this way, my learning at NALA was of a different and deeper quality, unexpected and unknowable at first. I arrived with the seeds of radical education in my pocket, certain the lessons I had learned in my life as a Coady person would be needed by all. I, some wandering purveyor of critical pedagogy, would travel throughout the land scattering the transplanted learnings and metaphors of personal transformation and critical consciousness from my old home in Nova Scotia. Had I been paying enough attention though, I might have noticed this was an occupied knowledge scape, full to bursting with its own stories of adult education and transformation, of critical pedagogies emerging from its own shared tapestry. I believed I had come to teach, only to soon realize I had arrived to be taught. I had been assigned truly deep work, work that belonged in this technological century, work that spoke of networked algorithms of adult learning: processes of criticality, possibilities of connectivity and programs of creativity. This cubic complex of criticality, connectivity and creativity became my new lens for inquiry and pedagogy. It beckoned me to examine my practice as an educational technologist and adult educator, bringing these disparate selves into communion — threads intertwined and tied off, cast on the loom of my life's tapestry, ready to be added to the patchwork of experience, thought and relationship (and a little magic) that has formed me as a radical adult educator.

Criticality – The Sage

I'm speeding down the Naas Road heading toward Newbridge to visit a place that applies a whole organization approach to critical pedagogy. My guide for the day, Blathnaid, is driving too fast for my taste — not that I don't like speed, but every turn of the conversation takes us significantly deeper into theory and related reflections about practice, and I'm already working hard to keep up. I'm clinging to my seat metaphorically and literally, as we sink deeper into a discourse around pedagogy and criticality — the heavy, Frankfurt school kind. Marx and capital, the eurozone and collective politics, Freire[1] and hooks[2], old struggles giving way to new identities, regression and evolution in Ireland. These pass in and out of the conversation as each topic is brought back to bear on the ways in which we change ourselves and our communities through informed and grounded capacity building and adult education: how 'we make the road by walking it.' I'm well used to these terms, and they sound right, but it's starting to feel that in recent years I've forgotten why.

We arrive and I initially struggle to place the heart of the organization. I'm looking for a shiny strategy document or program prospectus, but instead I'm surrounded by the softly glowing, lived fuzziness of applied strategy. I'm looking for the educators, but the label defies simple analysis here. They are all educators, just as bell hooks envisioned[3], and they, as educators take their lead from the learners, who in turn lean on the skills of the educators, who again in turn defer to the learners for clarity and collaboration around direction. Knowledge dances and loops here, working its way through all the lives it touches, bending a living pedagogy to its purpose rather than the other way. In a very counter intuitive moment for a radical educator, I feel like I'm an empty vessel being filled. But this isn't crude banking education of the sort Freire warned us against. I can see it now — the heart of the organization — and it's pervasive, it's in every hallway, classroom, lab and workshop.

I listen as a teacher warms a pot of tea, then instructs learners on service and amounts, and about the qualities of quantities when hosting colleagues, while carefully pouring and serving them. We all sit and eat and drink tea as Irish people have done for so long, and we all talk and listen, together. We eat and talk, and student and educator and administrator and visitor blend, telling stories about how learning is infused throughout the whole organization, how all of us contribute to each other, how as learners and educators, we are always with each other. Here, practice is entirely infused with theory, and living theory is emerging from every learning experience.

My soul is on fire as I note how critical pedagogy in its truest sense is woven throughout the organization. The staff are awakened to the potential in every person and every learning moment, and it becomes clear to me for the first time in a long time that critical, liberatory education isn't about theorizing, analyzing the learner or the program. It's about continuously making the world we long for in our living practice — a world that champions lived experience alongside grounded theory. One that seeks a better way not because it's marketable or current, but because it's what's left after we stand with the learner and apply the lens of their lived experience along with the theorizing and conceptualizing of our trade as radical educators. This organization is in a perpetual state of critical consciousness and everyone here is actively engaged in pruning and caring for it. I leave the place a changed educator, washed and rinsed in the criticality of the moment. I'm eager for the speedy return journey with a deep smile and a sense of engaged calm. I'm coiled in this new thread. I will untangle it and weave it into my own fabric, carrying it with me as I continue on my journey.

Connectivity – The Teacher

I spend most days in the office in awe (and occasionally, a little shock) at the generative powers of my office mate, Helen. I've simply never met a person who can create and craft innovative thought so wildly and so solidly at such a ferocious pace. Admittedly, it's frustrating at times. I have work to do, but I'm completely compelled to sit and engage: not out of any duty to politeness or social grace — Ireland doesn't suffer such trivialities well. No, I'm compelled to absorb this deluge of knowledge and experience and innovation more like a student listening to a professor they really admire, but who has also left last night's assignment to be completed in class. It's a curious blend of imperative and expectation, with just a small amount of fear. To be clear, in my arrogance I've often considered myself a reasonably quick and coherent thinker, but this is a qualitatively different sort of thing. Every topic we broach, she cracks open like an over-ripe watermelon, spilling forth a myriad of seeds, ideas and concepts. Some are instantly actionable and seem like they might be interesting projects. Some ideas arrive with a built-in bibliography, as she pitches books and articles at me from a seemingly inexhaustible library. And some are deeply practice oriented, tasking me with incorporating new mechanics and facilitation approaches immediately into my work with learners. I'm furiously writing down idea after idea, and my notebook is filling up far too fast.

Fridays are the best. It's a quieter day in the office, and Helen often brings me a strong coffee after lunch to help survive the afternoon. We begin to unpack critical learning, critical thinking, critical approaches to literacies of various kinds, critical program design. I grow more aware the key thread in all of this is a unique type of connectivity she keeps pointing out — a critical connectivity, an action-oriented approach to learning aimed at consciously interacting with the connection between people, understanding how to locate the pathways along which social, cohesive change can flow and fill community.

We unpack the idea of connected critical literacies, of building a lens from critical theory and utilizing the tools of critical thinking to interrogate the concepts of multiple literacies in shared learning spaces. The thread forms and I grab hold of the realization that criticality must never assume community, but rather must explicitly define connection as a key component in radical pedagogical design. Connection is so central to our existence that we've come to assume it's also automatic in our critical analysis, but that isn't always a given in a neoliberal society that champions the individual over the collective. Connection is the precursor to collaboration. Connection prompts us to always ask who is at the end of this thought, this intervention, this program, this design. Connected criticality becomes even more crucial in our analysis when we consider the networked technological substrate that underlies much of modern Western society. In a world where we are connected 24/7 by the shiny-screened devices in our pockets, connected criticality asks us to consider the ripples of causality that emanate from our work as community educators, and how the initial conditions we set will invariably shape and constrain learning far beyond anything we have a direct impact upon. Learning can become viral now, moving along its own digital pathways, ones we must strive to better understand and engage with as radical adult educators. I loop this thread, tying its ends together, and will run it through my fingers, feeling its complexity and its endlessness, how it encodes the beginning and end as one and neither. I weave it into my own fabric and carry it with me as I continue my journey.

Creativity – The Thinker

I'm immediately comfortable working with Tina in a way I had forgotten about; she's from my 'side' of Dublin and in such perfect Dublin fashion is so utterly unembarrassed to gently remind me of where I come from and how much of it still lives in my bones. We are designing research together and I become aware that for the entire train ride to our destination, I've been working hard to give life back to my Dublin accent, both literally and figuratively: certainly not to impress her, but to assure her I'm still worthy of the title 'Dub.' Dublin: a city where my family can trace its history for an age; a city that was unkind and kind to me in even measures, and how I love it so much for that grounded and grounding education; a city that can test even the most urban and woo even the most rural.

Our talk turns to the history of adult learning programs in the inner city, and we share stories of the deplorable public housing of the '70s, the heroin scourge of the '80s, and the fake prosperity of the '90s. We return again and again to the single mothers of working class Dublin and their presence in community organizations, with their

devoted and unending leadership and drive for relevant and affordable creative platforms during those various socioeconomic trials,
those 'belles' that have guided and championed a city's children to
envision and construct a community of their own design. Our story
sings the same song, but Tina is a headliner and I'm a backup singer.
She is a single Dublin mother and I'm the child of one – and here,
in our sharing I'm witness to her story. It is one thread in the fabric
created by generation after generation of Irish women community
leaders, building castles out of cardboard so their children might just
not notice, might just miss the ceiling of poverty and class oppression
that seeks to define and destroy them. Women leaders and educators,
my own mother among them, that are insatiably curious and committed to seeing to it that people enjoy community that is enriching,
uplifting, soul-nourishing and mind-building – money be damned.

This thread takes hold of me, and I begin to contemplate the crucial
role of feminism, of bell hooks and critical literacies, and the key
role of creativity in liberatory and radical community education. To
build away from the subjecting forces of hegemonic ideology, creative
dissent and an artistic, joyously generative energy must be honed and
tempered, turned toward the creation and adaptation of new language
for equitable and inclusive communities. To remain critically engaged,
our pedagogical constructs must be those of a 'Dublin Ma' creating castles made of cardboard. Creativity fosters agency and thrives
on inclusivity, spawning reflective, critical learners. This is central to
removing the weighty expectations of class determinism. With creativity as our ally, we can chart a course that steers away from prevailing
oppressions and seeks new and liberating lands yet unseen. That is,
creativity allows us to open the space to collectively envision and enable
truly novel approaches to community learning; ones which the hegemonic frameworks of neoliberalism have yet to anticipate and as such,
have no defense for. Just as we all learn always, we can all create always.
It's not a precious resource that needs to be capped and carefully
distributed — it is a lightning bolt, generated in the heavens of our free
minds, that tears through expectation and renders ideological platitudes
helpless. I will wind this thread around my finger, thumbing it for
safety when the demons of doubt arise in my own practice as an educator of critical, creative community engagement. I add it to my tapestry
and will carry it onward in my own journey as a light for others.

Making a New Road

"We make the road by walking it" is one of the foundational notions in radical, liberatory adult education pedagogy and practice. I've said it out loud many times over the years, even pontificated about it on a number of occasions. But I'm now unsure if I've ever truly understood it. Now it seems less about responsive program design, less about participatory facilitation or of critical analysis and 'post various this and that' theories. Now it feels like it's alive and moving, threads woven through my practice and intellect, grafted onto my spirit, and bound to my lived experiences. The road may lead to wherever we intend, but it is very much crafted from those materials we commit to the effort. If they are only ever conceptualized and theorized, they will be brittle and inflexible, susceptible to cracking and fragmenting. But if they are true and authentic, rooted in the dreams and aspirations of communities, they will be living, like green wood — strong and pliable — and they will grow and evolve to become difficult to uproot, supportive and reliable. They will lay underfoot and provide creative, connected stability and a true critical direction.

This road we make is the only pathway across time toward promise and change and a better tomorrow for all. And there can be no mistake, we make it together. In Ireland, my friends at NALA helped me to remember this. The threads I carried from the Coady have moved across the globe with me. They were found at the bottom of my pocket while I rummaged around looking for the familiar sadness that a wounded soul provides. I carried them with me, returning them for recharge and reworking in this city of my birth. My colleagues at NALA lent the required Irish threads to rebuild and reintegrate them into my tapestry as an educator, and I safely stowed them away with me for my return to Nova Scotia.

Endnotes

1   Paulo Freire lived and worked in Brazil to eradicate illiteracy among people from previously colonized countries and continents. His insights were rooted in the social and political realities of the children and grandchildren of former slaves. His ideas, life and work served to ameliorate the living conditions of oppressed people. His best known work is Pedagogy of the Oppressed. (1989). New York, NY: Continuum Publishing.

2   bell hooks is an American author, professor, feminist and social activist who addresses the intersectionality of race, class, and gender in education.

3   hooks, b. (2003). Teaching Community: A pedagogy of hope. New York, NY: Routledge.

*Kalimba, gardening,
dance, drama, drawing
games and quilts and play -
work. We have spoken. Pre
verbal poets. Embodied.*

*I felt it
in my body. Stuck
at it.*

*The change came
slowly. Had to tackle
my own demons. No idea
what I am talking about
as yet but
I sense it.*

*Earth movers. Resonance -
connected to art and
knowing and insight.*

*Freedom to
be something other
than prescribed. To be
still.*

*Which side of the paintbrush
do you use? Art may allow
coherence but only if
you
serve
it.*

*The role of the circle is
to protect the lamb.*

*This is an invitation. Remove
the language. Play with
zippers. Dance vermilion. Sand
radiata off-cuts. Include. Write
something - about trees, about
pastoralism, about peace.*

Surprise. We have spoken.

nanci lee

From Contributions On the Transformative Power of Arts, Learning
and Teaching for Transformation E-Dialogue (University of Sussex, IDS,
written during my time as a Senior Program Staff at the Coady Institute).

Art for Change

*We cannot but be impressed with the spirituality
and the ethereal nature of the abstract thoughts
and the artistic dreams and visions of which the
human mind is capable. Those great ideas and creations,
especially of the artistic geniuses, have
inspired people during all the ages.*

Rev. Dr. Moses Coady
Masters of Their Own Destiny, 1939

Twelve

Art for social change and transformation

John Milad Gad, Egypt

I believe art is the lie that enables us to perceive the reality. As a theatre director and art therapist, born and living in Egypt, I have been using art to work with people in community for nearly 20 years. I especially work with marginalized groups, victims of violence, and refugees from different parts of the world. Here is my story and what I have learned.

My Journey

From an early age, while growing up in a comfortable family, I watched my mother support women in need in our community. She was often fighting for their rights. She was a role model for me, and it's not surprising that 90% of the people I work with now are women.

I graduated from a Faculty of Applied Arts in Egypt and then worked for an advertising company for five years as a graphic designer before giving it up to devote myself to art for social change. My passion for how art can create change for people and society prompted me to follow this dream.

I recognized that art can show how people feel and how they are suffering, often quietly. It's not good enough to tell people to pray and things will be all right; or that they can simply pray their way to an abundant life, and also be treated as full citizens with rights. Social change happens in the streets and I decided that's where I needed to be.

To accomplish my dream, I started participating in many workshops in Egypt and abroad focusing on art and human rights. For example, I learned a lot in an environmental rights workshop, and one on liberalism. Next, I travelled to a choreography workshop in Tunisia, which led to a drama and freedom workshop in France. My pathway has been very eclectic and has shaped my unique philosophy for using art, especially theatre, in working for social change. I call it Art for Social Change and Transformation (ASCT).

The Emerging Philosophy of ASCT

It is my belief that human beings have the capacity to figure out their destiny and find solutions to the life problems they face. They can also discover their life's purpose when given a space to reflect and admit their inner thoughts and feelings. In sessions I facilitate, the main idea is to help people discover the power they have within to heal themselves. I help create the space for people to discover what inspires them in their experiences, memories, pains, dreams, moments of light, and potential.

In this essay, I will describe the process that has evolved in my work with people from different nationalities and groups living in Egypt. I do this work with members of a theatre group I founded called WeLessa which means "there is still more." As a theatre troupe, we tour Egypt and visit the poorest villages to perform and offer workshops aimed at introducing people to ASCT. We continue to learn from these experiences in seeing how art can introduce and focus people on their human rights.

While on this pathway to social change and human rights, a staff member at the Canadian International Development Agency in Egypt, who had seen some of my community workshops, invited me to participate in a workshop on Active Citizen Engagement in Cairo. It was here I tested some ideas in using ASCT. I introduced some short films to provoke change among the participants, who were all social change agents like myself, and received helpful feedback.

All this was before the Egyptian revolution in 2011. When it came, it did not stop me. I continued to use art to help people effect change and regain freedom because I knew the power of art to touch people's feelings was faster than any political speech. The revolution in Egypt tore apart families and communities. There was a lot of violence, pain and fear. So, I began encouraging people from different cultural backgrounds, political leanings and religious beliefs to come together to exchange their life experiences through art and dialogue.

From 2010 onwards, I continued my own learning by participating in courses offered by the Coady International Institute: one in Egypt focusing on *Transparency and Accountability in Governance*, then a certificate course in Canada on *Advocacy and Citizen Engagement*, and another on *Communications and Media*. All these courses were filled with practical ways to promote important causes and helped me reflect on what we were doing in Egypt during the uprising against Mubarak and its aftermath. I consider these certificates to be a turning point in my life's journey.

What is Art for Social Change and Transformation?

ASCT is a creative method of expression that works towards changing personal perspectives, managing our behaviours and feelings, and improving self-esteem. ASCT is also used to observe changes taking place in our societies. This kind of engagement in art enables people, through the use of simple art tools, to express themselves; to nurture their capacity to change themselves and their society through a balance of art and psychology. ASCT helps people learn to know and accept themselves, as well as to learn new ways to interact without the interference of psychological complications.

Opening a Space to Share Pain

There is a particular sequence I use in group settings to help people open up to each other and trust the process. It starts with activities aimed at enhancing participants' creativity and introducing themselves. Next, participants are asked to dramatically re-create a single scene that reflects an aspect of their lives. The healing quality of music is used to awaken and remind people of their experiences and memories. Participants are asked to write their life stories and are encouraged to read their story to others. With 20-30 people in a group, many different stories are told. Those listening gently ask for more information or details that can enable the storyteller to pinpoint any violence present in their story.

This process is used to open space. There are taboos in all societies and cultures that discourage people from speaking up about issues concerned with violence. Therefore, in the workshops a variety of techniques are used to encourage the sharing of stories. Specific activities that have proven effective are: discussions after watching a film; writing and presenting puppet shows; and working with clay to represent how feelings and emotions are moulded by situations and events. Using these art forms encourages participants to share their stories, and can actually give them feelings of joy, even while recounting painful experiences.

The ASCT Process

The ASCT process has proven to be effective in slowly leading participants to comfortably work with their emotions. They are given enough time to process any thoughts that may cause themselves or others harm in the context of their lives. This particular methodology creates both an open space to build trust among participants, as well as it promotes privacy for the individual participant's story. In the process, to help participants recognize violence in situations, we introduce a psychodrama activity. In this, real life situations are re-created, then acted out. Other participants share their feelings and ideas as they watch the situations unfold. This helps everyone understand the circumstances they have been part of, and to consider how they could have acted differently to change the outcomes.

To summarize the ASCT process, we use three phases, each taking its own time depending on the group, to address violence in its many forms. The three phases are:

1. **Self-expression:** focusing on helping participants open up and discuss issues they may not have been accustomed to talking about before.
2. **Reflection and Evaluation of Concepts:** guiding participants through their own thoughts, related directly or indirectly to violence they have experienced, helping them to reflect on their perspectives and concepts.
3. **Inner Healing:** starting a process of healing, associated with the repercussions of being either the survivors or perpetrators of violence.

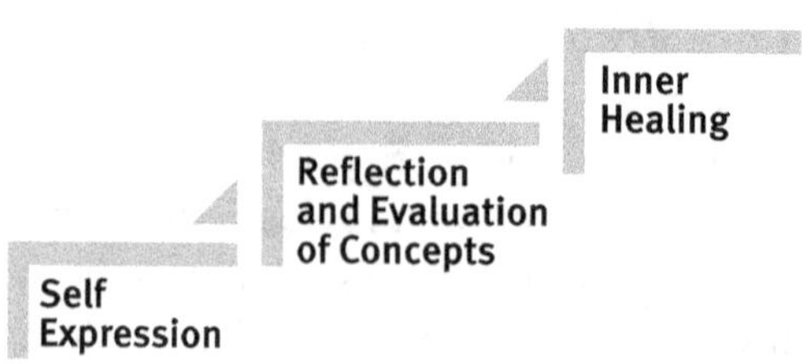

I understand pain is a part of life, but it's not all of life. I use art to help make change happen in society and create peaceful relations to make a better world. I encourage participants by telling them I will not be following up with them after the sessions. I tell them I have given them the tools to be a teacher and healer within themselves, to face all their problems. As one young woman said after being involved in workshops and performances, "You have taught me many things: I learned how to feel comfortable in my body, how to feel free, how to encourage myself, how to listen to good music, how to dance with the music, and how to know my feelings."

Forming WeLessa

Almost 20 years ago, I founded the theatre troupe WeLessa. The troupe uses the ACST model to support people in need in communities around Egypt. It may be with street children affected by violence, with refugees now living and working in Egypt, or with women experiencing traditional forms of violence in the family.

WeLessa conducts workshops customized for particular communities, which then culminate in an art performance developed with the workshop participants for an audience in their own community. These productions take a long time and much effort as the participants become the actors. For the girls among them, it is especially difficult to learn how to use their bodies and dance freely to express their pain and oppression. It is very important to break through this shyness first, especially as it is often the first time for many of them to be on stage. It's not easy for them to speak openly about the oppression they face every day in their homes, schools and universities, but it is part of my work as an artist for social change to give them psychological, as well as theatre training, so they can do this. I believe oppression is one of the worst forms of corruption in our Eastern Mediterranean societies.

The performances are the product of a number of different workshops for writing, dancing, singing and improvising. I prefer to make plays based on what people are facing and telling, rather than ready-made plays, because this kind of theatre paves the way for energetic youngsters to express themselves and discover their talents. Silence is one of the most serious crimes that society commits against its people. For example, when a girl is being sexually harassed on the street, no

one defends her. In fact, people might simply laugh at her plight. In
our workshops, we enact the suffering of sexual harassment with a
special dancing sketch that shows the deep pain and estrangement felt
by any girl who suffers this terrible experience.

The world today is using art to effect change and to regain freedoms. I think this is the way for Egypt to change, especially as
education is so poor; it is the only way to penetrate people's feelings.
Through art, change will happen.

Tackling Social and Political Issues

WeLessa has produced numerous plays aimed at putting real life
injustice in front of people and engaging them to think about what
needs to change. One impressive play WeLessa produced is called
Eats, Drinks and Sings Out of Tune. It's about oppression, murder,
sexual harassment, hope, dreams and many other social issues we
have seen in our society. There is mental harassment, as well as sexual
harassment, which makes people lose the good nature they were born
with and start harassing others. Eats, Drinks and Sings Out of Tune
is acted using mainly bodily expression and dancing, with very few
words. Eastern Mediterranean societies do not often believe that the
body can be used to express and deliver a message without words. We
are showing and proving how important the body is and how it can
be a tool for delivering important messages. Our troupe won seven
awards for this play in Egypt.

Since the revolution, our troupe has been presenting plays tackling
political issues, such as Skoot Hanswat (Be Quiet, We're Going to
Vote). We toured in almost every governorate in the country with this
play to make humble people in remote areas more aware of the electoral process, and to think carefully before choosing their nominees.
Art is a very important method to deliver a particular message that
humble people can appreciate.

Another play started with a workshop where we trained people with
disabilities to express their demands with their whole bodies, including
sign language and more. The play was called Human Rights via Art.

One of the most impressive plays produced by our troupe is El
Sofara (The Whistle) that tells the story of a humble rural traffic police-
man who gets a fortnight holiday. The play revolves around the last 15
minutes of his holiday, before he goes back to work, as he reviews all

the negative things that have been happening on Egyptian streets. At the end of each performance of this play, we give the audience whistles and tell them to whistle when they spot a violation, as a way of saying no. We have performed this play more than 30 times in Egypt.

Our plays always try to spread the idea of freedom and non-discrimination based on religion, gender, ideas, ability and/or skin colour.

Custom Designing for Diverse Refugee Communities in Egypt
Over the past years, I have been asked by international NGOs to work with them, using ACST, in some of their programs organized for refugee communities in Egypt. There are many nationalities and ethnicities in Egypt — Oromo, Eritrean, Ethiopian, Somali and Sudanese. As WeLessa, we use the same model, but each time it is adjusted according to the nature of the group. Some groups accept dancing, others benefit when clay and toys are used; for others, it can be writing or singing that helps them break their taboos. It is always important to consider their nature and background. Each workshop is customized according to the group in terms of how we start, the activities we use, and sequence of activities that evolve. Our plan is to have several get-to-know-each-other activities to start, and by observing the responses of the group during the first 15 minutes of the first session, we can then figure out what is needed for the remainder of the workshop.

Our target is to open people to how art can change their lives and how we can make peace and freedom part of our society. Our work is fun, but not just fun; it is also a medium to create a better world.

Up to now, we have worked with more than 16,000 refugees in Egypt in workshop settings. The length of each workshop varies between five to ten days, depending on the supporting organization and the people in the groups. Each group will have between 25-30 participants. Female Syrian refugees are known to face much violence in their lives, more than any other group of women we work with. Their stories include being beaten, treated badly by the husbands' families and abused in many ways. We have witnessed the most dangerous part of their situation is that they accept this as normal. We observed it is very hard for them to talk and express their feelings about these situations. Syrian participants tend to escape from their own stories of personal pain and violence by talking about the war. After being involved in our sessions, many of the women began reporting the violence they experience to police.

We realized how important it was to also have sessions with the men to give them outlets to express themselves, breaking the societal pressure that pushes them to suppress their emotions. These opportunities are extremely important to male participants and their families, as they offer an alternative to violence, which the men have not been exposed to before.

When we do this work in a distinct community, where it is considered normal for men to be dominant and women to feel disempowered, we must create space where both women and men are present so women can speak up in ways they have never been accustomed to with men around. This also gives men the chance to see women in a different light. In the spaces we create, all are equal. With very little direct interaction between women and men within the community, this type of session creates a unique platform for everyone to address and see each other differently. This then gets translated into interacting differently with each other in the gendered roles they play out in their daily lives.

The United Nations High Commission for Refugees is one of the organizations we partner with, and they tell us they observe changes and healing in the women. They also see it as a best practice that brings results in the living conditions for Syrian refugees in Egypt.

One special series of workshops for men only involved tuk-tuk drivers in Cairo and was supported by the United Nations initiative, Safe Cities. It wasn't easy to convince the drivers to take part in the workshops, but by the end of the training, most were convinced girls and women have the right to a safe environment, free of violence and harassment. I realized the workshop had been a success, and the message of peace had gotten through, when the wife of one of the drivers sent us a message to thank us and a gift she had made herself. She said she was thankful because now her husband buys her flowers and gifts, instead of beating and humiliating her.

I travelled with the United Nations International Child Emergency Fund to Sudan, where the focus was on defending freedoms. In Somalia and Ethiopia, we trained children in storytelling, dancing, writing and drawing. I work with youth and children in the streets and in villages. These are the people who will make change happen. I believe real democracy will not be achieved by politicians. It must come from the people, especially those who are marginalized. Workers and people living in the countryside, the poorest in Egypt, are the heroes in the plays we perform. WeLessa also recognizes the audience as heroes. We believe we are meant to be different from each other and to live together united, without bloodshed and conflicts, as God wants us to be.

A Moment with President Obama

I had a special opportunity to have WeLessa's work recognized by President Barack Obama. After we met, he told the audience, "Like all Egyptians, John has lived through the turmoil of recent years. As an artist, he uses his poetry and performances to help people discover the power inside them, which is as good a description of being an organizer as anything and being a leader. And he has been working to help women and girls recover from violence and sexual assault. He has focused on how to teach Egyptians to accept each other and he has said that we have rights that we can achieve in a peaceful way. John is the future."

This meeting with Obama came via the US embassy in Cairo when they invited me to participate in the International Visitor Leadership Program exchange called Stand with Civil Society held in the USA. During the 10-minute meeting prior to Obama's address, I told the US President my opinion on Washington's Middle East policy, which I think takes the side of government, not that of the people.

I said, "What a wonder; a year ago I was demonstrating and raising a placard reading: 'Obama, say sorry' and 'America is the graveyard of freedoms,' and now I'm standing and talking to you." I was astonished by Obama's reaction. He smiled and said, "This is life and different people should become friends and try to understand each other." He added that political life is always about change. I told him that Egyptians are refined people, yearning for freedom, and not like the Western stereotype of camel riders living in the dark ages. I believe Egyptian people are able to decide for themselves what their future will be.

The Future

I believe art, especially theatre, can be a vital tool for defending citizens' rights at this critical time. Theatre could tackle and discuss every aspect in life, not only social or political issues. Theatre could be considered a microcosm of our lives. So, I've started work on another dream — to create an organization that produces plays and other art, while training people in families and communities to work with children and teenagers. The purpose of offering this training is to give people tools to change their lives and society by means of art and psychology, teaching them how the individual can get to know and accept the self, and interact with others without psychological complications.

I refuse to leave Egypt and settle in another country. I love Egypt more than anything else in life. I want to stay here and continue working to change society for the better. After years full of violence and bloodshed, Egypt is ready to become an environment for healing. The violence perpetrated against people makes them feel that killing is normal, whether it is killing in the name of God or defending the country. When we start killing each other, we become inhuman.

Security is really important, and art for social change can happen anywhere as part of the solution when we, as facilitators, create safe spaces where people experience inner peace.

Images from our work can be found on this book's webpage at
www.pdltd.net/sprouting-seeds-of-radical-education
Point your smartphone camera at the QR code to link you directly to those images.

Thirteen

Transforming the meaning of inclusion

Lazarus George Udayakumar, India

Inclusion, based on my experience and observations in India, is an illusion. It is a widely used and often repeated word that relates to bringing diverse marginalized groups into mainstream society. In India, they can be marginalized because of their caste, class, religious, ethnic or sexual orientation or just about anything. The word inclusion is used by many organizations around the world, including the disability movement; unfortunately, people affected by leprosy are usually excluded. With their deformities, they have been treated as social outcasts since Biblical times and into the 21st century. This is prevalent in all countries that battle with this excluding disability. India accounts for 60% of the new cases reported globally each year and is among the 22 global priority countries that make up 95% of leprosy cases, warranting a sustained effort to bring the numbers down. In 2007 there were 137,685 new cases detected in India; this remained almost the same at 135,485 in 2016.[1]

People affected by leprosy experience physical, mental and emotional disabilities. Scarred, they lose their identity and dignity, and often lead reclusive lives. Many beg on the streets to survive; some find shelter and eke out a living. Many who have held positions in society before being afflicted by leprosy silently slip away to find refuge in sanatoriums or shelter homes when they are diagnosed, and are often disowned by their families. They withdraw within themselves and, in doing so, extinguish their light. They die unsung, unwept and unseen. Such is the tragedy that is hardly visible to society.

This story of transformation is about one such excluded community in the southernmost part of India at Kanyakumari. The story describes what transpired over five years, covers more than 18,000 km., spans three continents, involves three Coady

International Institute graduates and a few other friends, who all came together to create an art school for leprosy afflicted families and people with disabilities so they could find new meaning in life.

The Beginning (The Seed)

For my last elective in the 2014 *Diploma in Development Leadership* at the Coady, I chose Communication and Social Media. As I was walking out of the much-loved coffee room heading to the classroom David Fletcher, the Director, Educational Programs, appeared out of nowhere. He stopped me and asked what elective I'd chosen. When I told him, he pointed out with a quizzical smile, "Lazarus, as a performing artist, shouldn't you be part of the Art for Social Change course?" Before I could even blink Sr. Flavia, my close friend and a member of my Home Group, appeared and, with her Mother Superior's commanding smile said with authority, "Lazarus, I want you to join my group in Art for Social Change." So, you see I had no choice but to give in to David and Sr. Flavia who won me over with their compelling love. I was in the class the next day. There I learned how all forms of art — visual, literary, performing, even culinary — could be used effectively to motivate and create social change in communities, improving and transforming lives through this method of experiential learning. Our learning sessions were practical and interactive. Looking back, I am surprised how this course came to play such an important role in my life later.

Formation of the Team

In February 2015, I received a friend request on LinkedIn from Merlin James, an experienced social worker from Nagercoil, a town 700 km. south of Chennai, the capital of Tamil Nadu State in southern India. She discovered I had been to the Coady and wanted to find out more about it. We became close friends, meeting in Chennai and later Nagercoil, where she was involved with the Stella Maris Institute of Development Studies, to start working on projects. She would provide information about the needs of the people and the required data while I would prepare funding proposals and applications for grants. When Merlin expressed her desire to participate in the Coady's *Global Change Leaders* (GCL) program, I rejoiced like an evangelist who had converted "one more soul," and promised to do my best to help her. Soon after, she became the CEO of Stella Maris Institute of Developmental Studies at Kanyakumari, headed by Sr. Dr. Archana Das. Merlin brought the three of us together in a triangular friendship so we could explore ways to work collectively as a team. There was something special about this new friendship but I did not know then what role it would play in this story. When Sr. Archana and Merlin later also became graduates of the Coady, this forged a new bond among us.

The Flash Link

I have been involved with Agape Life Line Trust, an NGO based in southern Chennai since 2012. It works among leprosy affected people in a sanatorium that dates back to 1864 at Chinglepet, a town 70 km south of Chennai. Today it is India's Central Leprosy Teaching & Research Institute. We visit those getting treated in the wards and residences and provide things such as soap, toothpaste, biscuits, pickles and other Indian snacks which they don't get.

While I was there in 2016, I came across a newspaper article about the work of an Austrian artist, Werner Dornik who with his wife Dagmar Vogl, started an art school for leprosy affected people next to a home for elderly affected people at Bharatpurum on the outskirts of Chinglepet. They visit each year to teach and to host art exhibitions that raise funds from the paintings the participants create. Beena Gilbert, the head of the NGO, and I met them at the art school. A surprise was waiting for us. People we used to meet in the hospital as patients greeted us as art school participants.

Werner told us all about their work, their struggles and how they manage today. I was truly impressed by his transformative work with leprosy affected people. There was a flash in my mind as I saw the possibility of replicating their work but didn't know where. Unable to contain my excitement about what I'd seen, I rang Merlin and told her about the art school like I was a kid in a toy store. She responded with equal excitement, saying, "Do you know we have a leprosy colony here in Stella Maris? Why can't we start an art school here?" I replied, "Why not!" That day laid the foundation for the art school at Stella Maris.

Trying Times and Breakthroughs

Unfortunately, we were unable to get anything done for two years as Sr. Archana was in Canada for the 2016 Coady *Diploma in Development Leadership*, Werner was on his annual home visit, and Merlin went to attend the Coady's *GCL Program* in 2017. On her return, Merlin got Sr. Archana's consent to start the art school, but we could not do anything as there was still no word from Werner, even after he and his wife returned to India in early December 2017. I kept trying to get in touch and waited for him to reply. Finally, the breakthrough came in late January 2018 when Werner contacted me to say he could spare two days in late February. That was enough for me to blast off. I informed Merlin and Sr. Archana to get everything ready at Kanyakumari for the Dagmar and Werner's visit. In the meantime, Werner and I discussed how to develop our art school and how I could ensure it was on track with regular monitoring and guidance, as his visits are only for a short period each year.

The High and Low

On 20th February 2018, Dagmar, Werner and I arrived by the overnight train from Chennai. Sr. Archana, along with Ninian and Carol, two volunteers from Ireland, received us. Merlin joined us later. It was the moment we had been waiting for — to open a new chapter for leprosy affected people in the area. Werner was given the floor to share the story of his art school and how it could work at Kanyakumari. There was a multimedia presentation and a display of paintings created by pupils at his school. He was enthusiastic about starting a new art school in Kanyakumari. That evening we interacted with people from the leprosy colony and talked about the benefits of the art school. It could train them to become artists and sell their paintings to give them an income as a livelihood option. It could bring about social change by turning them from being beggars into artists.

The next day, we discussed everything related to the running and development of the art school. Ninian and Carol, who were in charge of administration, did the talking for Stella Maris. Werner, Merlin and I promised Sr. Archana, Ninian and Carol that everything would be taken care of to create another art school on the lines of the one at Chinglepet: then we waited. Ninian and Carol, however, did not want the school to start immediately as they were returning to Ireland for a year. They wanted it to start after they returned so they could keep it under their administration. Merlin, Werner, and I were crestfallen. We tried to reason with them, but they were firm and there was nothing we could do.

The Detour

Werner was sad over the turn of events after all the hard work on his side, as well as mine. As the train rattled its way back to Chennai, his wife Dagmar and I tried to reason with him and asked him not to lose hope. It was during this conversation that he asked me to perform a two-hour concert for his art school pupils at Chinglepet. I accepted, but wondered — playing violin for two hours is a long time, how would I manage? Believe me, it was magical. Although I played for two hours non-stop, I experienced no fatigue playing Christian hymns and Indian music for that long. I was elated when I finally saw the lovely paintings the pupils created as they had listened and transformed the dynamic fluid music into colorful designs. I could see the flow of the waves of music in their designs, which stunned me. Werner later informed me he had posted the paintings and a story about the concert on the art school website.[2]

The Silence and Turnaround

Everything seemed to be forgotten after that visit in February 2018. Nothing was stirring, but I wasn't willing to give up my dream of an art school. It's not for nothing that my name is Lazarus!

A year and six months passed. Then one day in August 2019, a friend in Nagercoil sent me photos of a program she had attended. I was surprised to see Sr. Archana in the pictures. I forwarded them to her, and in the ensuing conversation she asked me to start the art school, even though Ninian and Carol had still not returned. That was the moment I was waiting for. It was the turnaround. Finally, on 16th September 2019, I landed at Stella Maris to start working on the art school. I met colony members to convince them the art school could provide them with a livelihood through art instead of begging. Fr. Belix, an art therapist referred by Werner, visited us and gave us ideas about how we could proceed.

Realizing the Dream

Our long-desired dream became a reality when the Stella Maris
Art School was inaugurated on October 24, 2019, by the Deputy
Director of Horticulture, Ashok Macrin. Sr. Archana organized the
event beginning with a prayer and blessings by Father Vincent. Sr.
Archana and I briefly shared the journey we traveled so far, our vision
for the community and the contributions of Merlin and Werner in
making it a reality. Thirty-five members of the leper colony took part
in the program including 20 women, two children and 13 men.

As soon as the formalities were through, the art educator Chandra
Babu from Lalit Kala Academy, Trivandrum Chapter, India's top art
academy, took over. Magic wafted through the hall as he demonstrated how to draw and paint. He went around to encourage
participants to paint even if they were holding a brush for the first
time. Those with disfigured limbs painted by holding the brush in
whatever way they could. The community hall was filled with excitement and palpable energy. The budding artists were coming out
blazing in all colours, bringing out their hidden talents. The energy
was electric. The participants painted landscapes, animals, birds, flowers, houses, trees and whatever they had in their minds (*Picture 1*).

Picture 1: Participant paintings from the first art class.

Their auras were glowing as if they had attained enlightenment. There was something magical about the whole exercise.

That evening the paintings were displayed in the hall for participants and a group of visitors. Everyone was excited to see them. Five paintings sold and the money was immediately given to those who had created them. Each painting sold at a flat rate of INR 500/$10 CAD, a decent price for a painting without a frame. We just could not believe what leprosy affected people and persons with disabilities could create. Colony members themselves were beaming to see their work displayed because they could not believe they had created it.

The Challenge

We were all happy and hoping to grow the art school on the momentum gained, but there was another challenge around the corner. The art school participants from the leper colony went back to their old ways of begging the very next week after going through those inspiring painting sessions. Although they had agreed to be in class every afternoon, only 15 to 20% of the members turned up. It was heartbreaking. I had to find out why.

I had a heart-to-heart talk with those who stopped coming to the school about the lure begging had over them. Their answers surprised me. Their earnings were equal to that of someone from the Indian middle class, averaging INR 30,000/$600 CAD every month. Then I knew what held them back: the money. I knew getting out of begging would not be easy with that kind of money to be had. It was the only diversion they had to forget their condition and the rejection of society; they saw no hope in the future. This helped me to understand and accept the mindset of the leprosy community even more.

Then I remembered what Werner had told me about what happened when they started their art school in 2005. He faced the same struggle — begging was the menace that brought attendance down in Chinglepet too. He managed to get them back with a monthly stipend of INR 2,000/$40 CAD shared equally by the Government of Austria and the Indian Council of Cultural Relations, a wing of the Government of India. I realized how difficult it would be in Kanyakumari, one of the most attractive tourist spots in India, where the earnings from begging would be much greater and steadier. This made me all the more determined to wean colony members away from begging with attractive options to choose art as a livelihood and to see the value behind it. I planned to provide stipends also and began enlisting individual sponsors. I continued to visit the colony in November and December to encourage them. Sr. Archana was there to back me up and it began to work. Members came and sat for two hours to draw and paint. Though fewer in number, it was steady. I taught the way the art therapist Fr. Belix told me. We celebrated Christmas on December 23rd with songs and a renewed spirit. Colony members promised to come regularly from January 2020.

State of Suspended Animation

With new plans for food provisions, a monthly stipend and exhibitions for the art school, I was all set to start again in mid-January 2020, but everything came crashing down when I fractured my right foot and was confined to bed for the next two months. Then COVID-19 came calling and everything went into lockdown. The pandemic left us in a state of suspended animation.

A year passed and so did the first wave of the pandemic. In March 2021 I decided to visit the colony to talk about painting again so they could earn an income instead of begging, which had been difficult during the pandemic. They agreed and just after I distributed painting kits to them, the second pandemic wave struck. This became a blessing in disguise because during this latest lockdown they are forced to remain in their colony and can create paintings that will be ready for sale once things open up again.

When I look back, I am struck with wonder about the way things have evolved and how different people have been involved at different stages. I had no idea at the time that my volunteer work with Agape Life Line Trust and the Coady's *Art for Social Change* course had planted seeds that would blossom into a platform for leprosy affected people and others with disabilities. Today we have an art school to help transform their status from beggars to artists, effecting social change through an inclusive process that, in the past, has often excluded them.

We don't know when we will be able to open the doors of the art school again, but we know we will rise again.

Endnotes

1 Rao, P.N., & Suneetha, S. (2018). Current situation of leprosy in India and its future implications. Indian Dermatology Online Journal, Vol. 9, no. 2, pp. 83-89. https://www.ncbi.nlm.nih.gov/pmc/articles/PMC5885632/

2 Art school pictures available at: https://www.bindu-art.at

— *Fourteen* —

Drawing on graphic dialogue to facilitate learning and change

Darren C Brown, Canada

I've been designing and facilitating learning for personal and organizational change for more than three decades. In fact, at the point in my young life when I confidently owned being called a "bookworm," I realized it's how I approach life, relationships and results. Designing and facilitating learning is my calling. Recently in my practice, I have been experimenting with graphic approaches to strengthening generative dialogue. A spectrum of trainings are offered globally and online to introduce and help increase the skill of graphic recording and graphic facilitation.[1] In many of these trainings, it seems developing a graphic practice that produces a final piece of visual art (practice for product) is at the core. However, my own practice has led me to conclude little has been explored in the realm of participatory graphic facilitation and recording as a learning process itself rather than a product. The word "participatory" has several inferences, but in this self-reflection essay, participatory aligns with the Antigonish Movement's Father Jimmy Tompkins' call to "restore the lost solidarity" across humanity.[2]

Through playful experimentation with graphics, I have observed in real time that with participatory graphic recording and immediate sharing, emerge creative and inspiring insights for learning consideration and reflection. I have also discovered the thoughtful use of colour, culturally relevant graphics and icons suggested (or created) by learners, as well as the insertion of short, accurate quotes can strengthen participation, advance dialogue, enrich team cohesion and enhance the inclusion of cultural diversities. Participatory graphic facilitation also holds the potential to induce a lot of laughter and liberating fun — a key element in creating a risk welcoming and innovative learning space.

This essay will explore six points of inquiry. Each point is based on a lived graphic facilitation experience and ends with a final note called

Drawing Out Learning. These observations and entry points can generate further learning inquiry and reflection.

Banishing "Oh, but I can't draw."
It is only fair to begin this learning reflection with owning a life-long self-oppression. Although attracted to colour and form, as well as drawing and sketching since childhood, I was afflicted by the same self-imposed or external judgments many of us have experienced — "That bird looks funny." "I've never seen a fish that colour." "Trees don't look that straight in the forest." The list is endless and the taunts are well known, as I expect they've been hurled upon anyone reading this essay. At some point, usually very early in life, the judgments by others begin, and one puts the pencil, pastel or paint away and owns "I can't draw."

The key to unlocking participatory graphic facilitation, recording or visualized thinking is banishing "I can't draw!" Everyone can draw, paint or create collages. Getting past fear and internalized oppression is the key.

There are plenty of online resources, workshops and recommended materials to initiate and inspire entry to the world of graphic facilitation, but I will not focus on technical aspects of graphic facilitation here. My own standard facilitator's kit always includes a pencil, a very basic set of chisel point markers and soft pastels. That's really all that is required to get started. As passion and interest grows, investing in an array of diverse and colourful tools might happen, but in starting, a small investment is sufficient.

The second enabler I have learned to make (particularly in multiple day workshops) is to provide a 45-60 minute micro-course in the very basics of graphic techniques and tools. I carry an extra graphic facilitator kit or two and leave them behind to encourage sustained inspiration and skill development of graphic facilitation inductees. Within that short time span, including a participatory experience to banish "Oh, I can't draw," participants can quickly pick up the key technical aspects of graphic facilitation and visual thinking. After that it's just practice.

> **Drawing Out Learning:** Teams and groups that learn together value and practice mutual reinforcement and collaboration towards achieving collective results. When introducing a graphics facilitation micro-course, it is rare

anyone in the participant group already has the skill set.
A levelling field is established. Individual and collective
humility enters the room. The learning environment is
fertile for both team learning and personal mastery.

Inviting "What do you see?"

What people see (or do not see) in graphic representation is the
entry point for commentary, discussion and dialogue for change. The
graphic image is the means to initiate curiosity, reflection and sharing — something concrete to facilitate discussion about rather than
judge the visual representation. For many, this requires a significant
mental model shift from the way we are socialized to view visual art.
Participatory and inclusive graphic facilitation is a means to learning, not an end in itself. This differs from the current trend for
graphic recording wherein a recorder (usually viewed as an 'expert')
visually captures the outputs of a dialogue process or workshop as a
permanent record of what transpired. In the latter case, the graphic
recording is the end.

For example, during an introductory graphics workshop with
an organizational team in Cairo, Egypt, while demonstrating how
to easily draw a simple human figure, my co-facilitator stepped up
behind me and quietly said, "Add a veil." No sooner had a quick
curved line been added to the head than a young man in the room
quipped, "Cool, a hoodie. I never come to these events and feel
comfortable wearing my hoodie … and there I am!" This provoked a
quick group discussion about why someone would think they could
not wear a hoodie, and progressed to an inquiry concerning assumptions and unstated biases (real or perceived) and socialized thought
patterns. The simple graphic actually initiated an entire dialogue-based
learning cycle on intergenerational assumptions, organizational culture
and hierarchies. Yet the original action was only to "add a veil!"

> **Drawing Out Learning:** The adage "a picture is worth a
> thousand words" could undoubtedly be termed a million
> words once an image is shared amongst a group of people.
> Our diversities and diverse life experiences frame our
> mental models and associations with pictures and visual
> images. Graphics provide an accessible entry point to

facilitate discussion which reveals diverse mental models,
ways of thinking and intercultural perspectives.

Co-Charting for Visual Clarity

How might an invitation to step up to co-charting and encouraging participants to "draw what they mean," embolden a shared vision and strengthen collective commitment?

Participants need encouragement and support to step into a graphic recording or facilitation role. It requires a very short micro-course coupled with a set of community learning values and principles that enable and ignite creativity and visual expression within a nonjudgmental space. In many ways this complements, and perhaps accelerates, the reflective dialogue phase of the generative dialogue process.[3] I believe as participants banish a previously held belief that "I can't draw" it further activates and liberates a whole new way of questioning previously held beliefs in self (and in others) as well as of organizations and systems. While experimenting with tools and colours and practising newly acquired skill sets, I have listened to participants laugh in camaraderie and delight. Quips like "You can do it!," "I love it," "Cool!," "Wow! I never thought of something like that!" spark community building and unleash collective creativity. As the community of learners is involved in a liberating shared experience it further kindles Father Jimmy Tompkins' call to "restore the lost solidarity" across humanity.

Once the powers of graphically inspired collective creativity, reflective dialogue and a mutually re-enforcing spirit have been unleashed, my facilitator role is simply to channel this energy towards achieving the shared outcomes of the day or the workshop.

An example of this emerged in 2014 during the post-Arab Spring period in Egypt. Convening a community of civil society organizations for the purpose of strengthening collective impact over a three-day workshop, a graffiti wall was co-created to capture reflections, key learnings and identify joint actions (*Picture 1*). The graffiti wall was a centering point for the community; everyone graphically contributed images, icons or words. Although initially proposed as a way to capture outputs, a strategic and shared vision emerged — one that garnered both shared commitment and was built on a solid foundation of experimentation, trust and creativity.

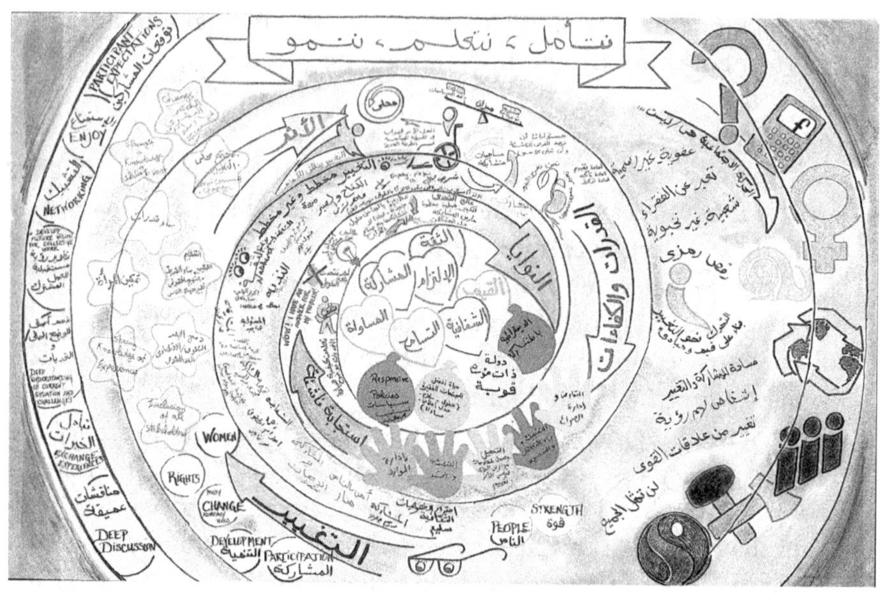

Picture 1: Graffiti wall on strengthening collective impact.

Drawing Out Learning: A shared vision amongst key actors is critical to achieving just and sustainable change. Too frequently, a community or organizational vision is discussed and wordsmithed to the extent that it can run the risk of polishing away the aspirational essence. At best the polished vision statement is hung on a wall to be read, at worst printed in a report and stacked away amongst piles of grey literature. A participatory process of drawing the vision on a graffiti wall, and then photographing and distributing for all participants to print letter sized posters, include in reports, project via PowerPoint or set as one's desktop image can sustain the life-giving essence of a co-created shared vision.

Strengthening Inclusion Amongst Diverse Cultural Realities

Why does the thoughtful use of icons and the most basic of graphic visualization training seem to transform and actualize inclusion amongst diverse cultural realities?

I vividly recall an insightful moment one autumn during Coady International Institute's *Learning Organizations and Change Certificate*

126

Program. I had arrived early to the learning space and posted a colour-fully inviting and graphically enhanced welcome sign, just outside the learning space. Shortly afterwards, the door awkwardly swung open and in rolled an enthusiastic participant from Uganda. She was in a wheelchair. I said, "Good morning and welcome. Are you looking for *Learning Organizations and Change*?" Her reply? "I am here for what-ever you are offering as I see I am included and welcomed in this space."

Similar to *Picture 2* below, I had drawn a person in a wheelchair on the welcome sign. I had previously noticed during my own graphic facilitation training, as well as in many graphic recordings, most human figures are able-bodied and I committed to shaking this up.

Picture 2: Close up of course welcome sign with inclusive image.

Drawing Out Learning: This example illustrates, like the veil mistaken for a hoodie in the earlier example, the powerfully welcoming and inclusionary spirit generated by a simple graphic or icon. Again, it serves as a very practical example of "A picture is worth a thousand words!"

Rapid Flipchart or Sketchbook Graphic Recording

When can rapid flipchart or sketchbook recording and immediate sharing increase internalizing learning and acting to change?

Many of us know the world of big wall graphic recording. The recorder captures what has been heard and renders it graphically during a one-day or multiple-day session. It can be as captivating as a magic show ... but it isn't magic! It's a trained skill, and once the tips and tricks are revealed, practice will make practically anyone comfort-able with their own graphic style. I started practicing and playing with the large format approach until a co-facilitator pointed out it might actually be distracting to the participatory learning process in the dialogue space. I paid attention to these words and observed that the large format graphic recording can trespass beyond a particular threshold to where the attention goes over to "What's next on the graphic?" or "How do you do that as the graphic recorder?" rather than remaining focused in the dialogue process at hand. Sketchbook graphic recording is an alternative.

In 2016, the University of Cape Breton launched the online course *Learning from Knowledge Keepers of Mi'kma'ki.* Live streamed, the course featured Elders of Mi'kma'ki speaking to particular themes of culture, history, health, well-being and politics. The course required reflection, ongoing dialogue and sharing on Facebook. For fun and practice, I started to sketch my learning from each session in a letter-sized sketchbook. In the spirit of sharing, I photographed and posted each sketch to Facebook. I was immediately struck by how many fellow participants wrote to appreciate the graphically captured and visualized learning of each two-hour session all in one place. It enriched post-session reflections as one could see the whole — somewhat like systems thinking or analysis. At the close of the course, having several completed graphics laid before me as a collage, I was able to see a unique Mi'kmaq world view or Indigenous perspective on lived reality. In short, the colourful collage was the portal for my own transformational experience of valuing 'Etuaptmumk' or Two-Eyed Seeing.[4]

More recently, in a five-day seminar in Brussels focusing on the European Green Deal, my co-facilitator and I took turns graphically capturing the plenary reflections on one sheet of flipchart paper, while the other facilitated the dialogue to generative reflection. We had established a little code, when the dialogue facilitator felt a particularly salient point had been reached, he would simply state something such as "catch this" and repeat or affirm the statement, indicating it should be graphically captured or recorded.

With a similar intention, in the Facebook postings of sketchbook recordings for future consideration and reflection, it was noted that participants frequently took photos of the flipcharts during breaks for memory recall and to enhance written reports and publications.

Drawing Out Learning: Systems thinking and analysis is enriched with real time production of infographics. Key to this is graphically capturing the entire system dialogue on one sketchbook or flipchart page. This enables participants

to see the distinct and specific parts, yet value that the parts
are only relevant within the context of the whole system.

Confluence During the COVID-19 Pandemic

What is being noticed about the transformative power of graphics to
consolidate network thinking and enhance human solidarity during
COVID-19, where we work from home in the online and virtual
space?

Hardships not overlooked, the early days of COVID-19 offered an
incredible portal to innovative network thinking and learning, and
graphics played a significant role in holding the intention of learning processes together. During the global pandemic, many facilitators
stepped up to invitations to work experimentally with committed
teams to migrate previously planned workshops and learning initiatives
into the virtual and online world while working from home and caring
for family and community. It was quickly acknowledged a two- or
three-day workshop could not possibly be rolled out over two or three
full days of Zoom room participation and sitting. As a result, learning designs were modified to achieve pre-COVID learning objectives.
There were several key elements in the success of platforming network
thinking and learning in the virtual space: an attention to thoughtful timing rather than allocation of time; intergenerational learning;
leveraging global time zones to optimize collective creativity; balancing
synchronous and asynchronous learning; and, of course, graphics![5]

As two- or three-day workshops were re-envisioned as a series of
90-120 minute dialogue-based learning sessions over a month or
more, it was soon realized a singular graphic image would best hold
the learning intention of the network or system together.

In a recent UN Food and Agricultural Organization (FAO) global
learning and networking pathway, *Microbiome: The Missing Link?*, a
singular graphic was collectively developed to illustrate a shared vision
of the process and outcomes of the pathway (*Picture 3*). About 100
participants, from a diverse technical range and global locations, were
involved in the pathway initiative. The graphic opened every Zoom
session to remind us of the journey travelled to that point, as well as
to position the current learning location. The graphic was like a map,
and upon reflection, its constant resurfacing served both to orient

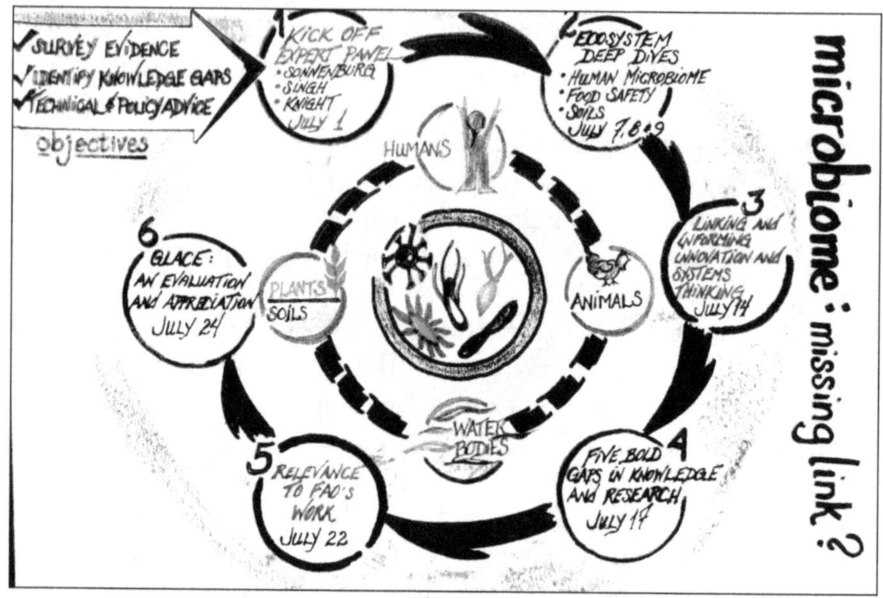

Picture 3: UN FAO shared vision of virtual learning pathway.

participants and build cohesion across the learning network.

Drawing Out Learning: A singular graphic illustrating learning intention and design kept network participants focused on the learning flow. The graphic was trusted like a chart of untraveled rivers as the diverse contributions of participants flowed in confluence to generate new insights and inspirations.

Drawing on Graphic Dialogue to Facilitate Learning and Transformation

In Pedagogy of the Oppressed, Paulo Freire shares, "Since dialogue is the encounter in which the united reflection and action of the dialoguers are addressed to the world which is to be transformed and humanized, this dialogue cannot be reduced to the act of one person's 'depositing' ideas in another, nor can it become a simple exchange of ideas to be 'consumed' by discussants. ... It is an act of creation."[6] This essay has explored participatory graphic facilitation and recordings, as a learning process itself rather than a product. It is based on experience, observations and reflections spanning a decade of practice. I have learned that enabling the diversity of others to graphically engage in dialogue strengthens the act of co-creation. I have witnessed it transform individuals amidst the very process of graphic dialogue, strengthening both their voice and their sense of belonging.[7]

Endnotes

1 I trained at The Grove Consultants International: https://www.thegrove.com

2 Correspondence from Father Jimmy Tompkins to Kingsley Brown Sr., 1933. Reverend James John (Father Jimmy) Tompkins (1870-1953) was a Roman Catholic priest who founded the Antigonish Movement, a progressive effort that incorporated adult education, cooperatives and rural community development to aid the fishing and mining communities of Northern and Eastern Nova Scotia, Canada.

3 Sunderland, K.R. (2012). Make Light Work in Groups: 10 tools to transform meetings, companies and communities. New York, NY: Incite Press, p. 71.

4 "Mi'kmaq Elder Albert Marshall of Eskasoni, Nova Scotia, in the Traditional Territory of Mi'kma'ki, coined the English phrase "Two-Eyed Seeing" many years ago for a guiding principle found in Mi'kmaq Knowledge as reflected in the language. One can see anything or any situation from both a western scientific viewpoint and a Mi'kmaq indigenous scientific viewpoint. The recognition and honouring of both viewpoints provides deep insights. Elder Marshall is a fluent speaker of Mi'kmaq ... Two-Eyed Seeing in his language is known as Etuaptmumk." Two-Eyed Seeing – Elder Albert Marshall's guiding principle for inter-cultural collaboration • Thinkers Lodge 60th Anniversary - Empowering our Climate Future for Rural Communities, 2017, Pugwash, NS.
http://www.integrativescience.ca/uploads/files/Two-Eyed%20 Seeing-AMarshall-Thinkers%20Lodge2017(1).pdf

5 Key elements in the success of platforming network thinking and learning in the virtual space will be further elaborated upon in the short essay Virtual Global Networking in the COVID-19 Pandemic in this book, p. 169.

6 Freire, P. (1989). Pedagogy of the Oppressed. New York, NY: The Continuum Publishing, p. 77.

7 High Resolution full colour images of the illustrations in this essay are available on the book's webpage at www.pdltd.net/sprouting-seeds-of-radical-education. Point your smartphone camera at the QR code to link you directly to the images.

Facilitation for Change

Fifteen

Our story of collective facilitation

Mary Ramsis, Nawal Ghatas, Cynthia Khoury, Victoria Morcos, Egypt

Before delving into our experiences and sharing our stories, we would like to tell you who we are and how we came together to weave our collective story. We are four female Egyptian graduates who studied at the Coady International Institute at different times and at different stages of our lives. We did not know each other before going to the Coady. Since returning to Egypt, we met in 2012 and again in 2014 as part of an active Coady Graduates Network, and we have become strong friends and colleagues.

Meeting like-minded people, specifically those who have gone through the Coady transformational experience, shortens the distance in getting to know each other. Briefly, we are:

- Mary Ramsis, a development practitioner working in international organizations and privileged to have initiated the Coady Graduates Network (CGN).
- Nawal Ghatas, an adult educator, a freelance development consultant and the founder of Haddouta Maereya Association (HM), which means Egyptian Tale.
- Cynthia Khoury, a freelance facilitator, a Scout leader, who left many years of desk work behind to follow a love and passion as a graphic facilitator, using skills and talents in the right place.
- Victoria Morcos, a passionate adult educator, counsellor and freelance consultant supporting people through charity activities, and co-founder of HM.

When we were asked to contribute an essay to this book, we got together and decided to write about our facilitation experiences. We each reflected on what we had learned about facilitation and shared written stories with each other. We reviewed each other's stories and highlighted key learning points. We saw so many commonalities about what was significant. From these, we were able to choose key points to share as practical examples of what we are learning about facilitation.

Two of the stories are about collective experiences we have had in the formation of HM, an NGO established in 2018, when several Coady graduates used their facilitation skills and tools to contribute to its set up and functioning. Our vision is a society that enjoys its humanity. Our mission is to provide opportunities for the existence of an aware humanitarian society, seeking life-long learning and constructive change through the implementation of development programs and projects with groups in poor and disadvantaged areas. Our core values are life-long learning, appreciation of diversity, participatory leadership, peaceful coexistence, and genuine humanity.

The other experiences shared here focus on joint activities in training and facilitation, which we conducted together in other organizations in the country as external consultants or volunteers, in-house trainers and/or partners. Most of the requests we received for facilitation focused on using Coady methodologies and the Coady magic of engaging and transforming participants. In other organizations, we provided safe spaces for their learning, reflection and organizational growth. These requests came from people who experienced the Coady's work from near or far, and requested help in influencing the changes in their organizations.

What Does Facilitation Mean for Us?

As mentioned earlier, we came together to write this collective essay by reflecting on our experiences of co-facilitation in different situations in a variety of organizations. Here we will share nine points with you about what facilitation has come to mean for us through our stories.

Facilitation is an Open and Free Space that Leads to a Fulfilling Experience

Nawal: As background to this story, it was in the summer of 2007 in a Coady course, when one of the teaching staff asked us to choose and design our own course. I immediately thought about my favourite topic: spirituality and transformative learning. With a lot of ambition, I presented and discussed this topic with diverse friends, who I thought could be interested in the topic. We became a group of eight people with our own classroom to work in. We gathered regularly, agreed on our own rules, assigned roles including facilitator among the group members, brainstormed ideas, let our conversation flow, created outlines, searched online, then designed and facilitated our favourite course. This experience is still alive inside me. It was an enjoyable, fulfilling and enriching experience in a perfect learning environment — full of love, peace and joy where everyone could be their own self. The approach aligned perfectly with my values. Since then, with that memorable feeling alive inside my heart, mind and soul, I apply it whenever I can.

An opportunity came in August 2014, when a group of us came together, mostly Coady grads, who still had the spirit of the Coady in us that is loving and appreciating each individual, whoever they are and whatever their background. Most of us obtained scholarships inside and outside Egypt to keep our learning journeys alive, and we consider it important for us to give back. Interacting with each other, we shared the same values. We also found we shared a common vision of how we could give back — we could start a small initiative to support girls in disadvantaged areas, both financially and emotionally, to continue their higher education. Each one joined the group willingly, with a passion to fulfil something that had meaning and matched their personal missions. We rekindled the spark!

The original group became the board and members of HM. At one of our regular meetings, we facilitated a reflection on their ongoing commitment to HM by asking, "Why do you still support HM? Is there anything different about it?" We established HM in a non-traditional way. It was with a spirit of love and appreciation that we created a free space for each one in our circle to play a voluntary role without compulsion. With the little we have, whether it was a donation of money or time, it was enclosed with love and appreciation for watching it slowly growing. We didn't rush the process. We let it happen until it became an entity for our wider community.

Here's what some members said:

"Together we planted a very small seed and we kept
watering it." (Mohamed, Coady grad 2016)

"We are a diverse family which comes from different governorates with different backgrounds and different cultures. This affirmed a genuine identity for the association and makes it unique and rich!" (Sherry, Coady grad 2008)

"HM is different, as it's a participatory association, built on a participatory approach to whatever happens within it." (Aida, Coptic Orphans Assistant Project Manager)

"Everyone has a space to voice their opinions either as participants or facilitators. Most of our decisions were made by consensus rather than voting. We feel ownership, talk our minds freely, any of us can bring others to join. Most importantly, as leaders we don't impose instructions on the participants but we are helping them to be themselves. There is not a dependency without awareness but a harmonious unity with awakened consciousness — together, the participants and ourselves are walking in a mutual learning journey. It is a journey of self-discovery!" (Salwa, Coady grad 2016)

"The association follows a participative leadership approach where all decisions, issues and problems are presented in full transparency in front of all members, so each member could make their decisions, with consensus, based on a clear vision." (Neven, Coady grad 2006)

"The more we dig deeper in HM values and our learning journey, the more we enjoy our humanity, the HM vision and our effective roles/existence. HM is a place where we become ourselves. It's a story to be told!" (Mariam, Coady grad 2007, 2013)

From the quotes above, you can see that a learning environment was effectively facilitated in the establishment and running of HM, full of love, peace and joy. As one of the HM founders, who experienced the open space in that Coady course back in 2007, I am very proud of how we set up a similar process, over a longer time frame for people in our own circle, who want to give back by creating opportunities for young women and girls.

Facilitation Listens to Everyone's Voice in a Safe Space with Appreciation

Nawal: I am grateful for having been exposed to many different approaches in facilitation that have become principles in my life, inside and outside my work. One of these approaches was originally used in a closing activity at the Coady, called the talking circle. In such a circle, a safe space is created for every participant to share their opinions freely, without expecting judgment from others.

I first witnessed this approach in the 2007 Coady diploma courses. I very much admired this activity and since then I apply it in every HM workshop, session and in my work as a facilitator in both non-formal and formal settings. Why am I using it so often? Because in our culture, everyone listens only to comment or judge. This activity grants each individual a chance to speak their mind without any judgment from the listeners or other participants. It provides a safe space for each speaker to talk from their heart, and in return knowing that their voice will be heard respectfully and attentively. It relieves the speaker from feeling tense or worrying about how people will respond. For the listener, it gives a unique opportunity to really listen without thinking of what they will say in response. One of the rules set out by the facilitator when the talking circle gets set up is to not comment or judge, even in your mind. We developed our own expression of this for our groups: "Listen without jumping to conclusions. Listen, just to let yourself go with the flow of the thoughts and words of the speaker, believing that they speak the truth from their heart."

Sitting in a circle became one of our main approaches in HM *(Picture 1)*. It is a space for all people to share — young, old, big, small, teen or adult. We would do a group activity with the young people at the end of each session, carried out twice a week, where the mentors and children sit together in a circle in a friendly learning environment. Here the young people and children in HM experienced a completely different kind of environment than in their school, where there is so much judgment and punishment. The children love being at the association, because as they express it, "In this place, there is only love, no punishment like in our schools."

Here is a testimony from one mentor, Asmaa:

> "She (the young girl I am mentoring) always gives me the feeling that I am a good listener, especially since she isn't much of a talker. It's very honouring to be her confidante. During one discussion she said, 'my responsibility is to spread love.' I used to think that to eradicate hatred we have to spread peace, but to spread love is very accurate and so beautiful, coming out of such a pure, innocent child."

The association also provided a safe space for the mentors to develop their talents. Yasmin is a student, majoring in History, who found appreciation and started to develop her writing talent to be more positive, capturing the touching moments that happen in the association among the mentors and the children. Here is a piece of her writing that expresses how the children feel safe in the association:

> "One day I found my daughter depressed and sad; she didn't have the motivation to do anything and I tried to deal with this as hard as I could, to finish what we were doing, but she told me something that made me think. She said, 'I know you'd never beat me for whatever I do and that's why I come here without being afraid of anything.' That moment I knew that my daughter had found and touched that safety feeling."

Picture 1: Sitting in a talking circle is a key HM approach.

Facilitation is a Communication Tool
Victoria: I am privileged to be a part of HM with people I love to
share with — our common values and our dream of a world having
a humanitarian image. It was a unique opportunity to achieve this
old dream of mine that I never thought would come true. Because
most of the co-founders of HM have the same mindset and same
experience at the Coady, we cherished the chance to apply the Five
Disciplines of the Learning Organization[1] when we established
the HM Association. Each one of us used their personal mastery in
performing their roles, respected the mental models of others, built a
shared vision, enjoyed team learning and adapted our system thinking in setting strategies and priorities. We built a comfort zone so as
to have fun in planning activities and setting budgets that could have
been very stressful in other environments. Through all these processes,
I experienced how to be more patient in communicating with people
who had different mental models. By including a wider meaning to
'respect' as a value, it extends respect to the timing it takes to create
shared understanding and in seeing another person's perception.

Adult Education is a Facilitation Approach
Victoria: Living at the Coady for more than five months meant
participating in rich courses on different themes. We interacted
with facilitators who had a unique taste and openness in their attitude. They were always welcoming our questions, comments and
were generous in their advice. Finding myself sharing daily life with
50 colleagues from 35 countries, who became friends, was a constant
learning environment. All these factors engraved new aspects into
my personality and my memory. It takes no effort to recall them.
Distance and time will never let my mentor, Olga Gladkikh — "the
power of love," as I call her — stop being generous in giving advice,
encouragement and support. This is one of the reasons I see myself as
my mentor sees me, pushing me to explore hidden talents that I never
thought I had.

Above all, I was overwhelmed with adult education and adopted it
as my philosophy on a personal level for self-reflection, and for ongoing learning in all aspects in my life.

My belief in adult education was strengthened when I applied my
learnings through counselling people in my community, especially

traumatized women. It was, and still is, a big challenge to enjoy day-by-day the fruits of the facilitation process itself. The quality of counselling and support I give to people has been transformed. This kind of facilitation allows the other person to feel safe, equal, comfortable to share their weakness, without stress or shame, because s/he is appreciated for themselves. I realized that to deeply apply adult education, I should understand others and I should create a virtue of tolerance in myself. Although I was, and still am a good supporter to others, in the past I would give solutions to the issue which resulted in a relationship of dependency with learners. Working with the experiential learning cycle,[2] the relationships became healthier and more independent by going through the phases of reflective observation, abstract synthesis and active experimentation. Referring to tolerance in an interview conducted at the 1996 World Conference on Literacy organized by the International Literacy Institute, Philadelphia, USA, Paulo Freire said:

> "In order to understand the others, I discovered that I
> have to create in myself a certain virtue without which
> it is difficult for me to understand the others: the virtue
> of tolerance. It is through the exercise of tolerance, that I
> discover the rich possibility of doing things and learning
> different things with different people. Being tolerant is not
> a question of being naïve. On the contrary it is a duty to be
> tolerant, an ethical duty, a historical political duty. It does
> not demand for me to lose my personality." [3]

Facilitation Starts with Accepting the Special Talents of Co-Facilitators and Participants

Cynthia: Here is a statement that really rings true for me and reflects how I feel about life: "Surround yourself with those on the same mission as you."[4] It is very difficult to work with people that do not understand you, your mission or your way of doing things. I worked for many years with people who thought I came from another planet! I was never passionate about my work … it was just a job. I felt very different than everyone else in those job settings and I didn't know why!

Now I understand that I was in the wrong place with the wrong people. Being different, however, gave me lots of good chances that I used thoroughly.

I have a passion to help children and youth grow and develop so they become useful to themselves and to their communities. From this they can take a constructive place in society as responsible citizens — which is how I was raised. For more than 25 years, I have been a Scout leader. Scouting is a progressive system designed to achieve goals. In Scouting, I was able to see and monitor the change happening in people. This was an amazing feeling because I then knew I was making a difference. That's why I believe in this quote by Lord Baden Powell, founder of the Scout Movement: "Leave this world a little better than you found it." [5]

When I was at the Coady, I joined several different courses and I discovered that I was a good facilitator — always had been — but I didn't know it! Being at the Coady and working with Coady people made me realize you can feed off the energy of those around you. Working alongside other professionals encourages a person to reach the next level in their career, as they learn new ways of thinking and get feedback from other like-minded professionals. That's why I decided to follow my passion, to do different work with love, and to use my facilitation talents in the right place. I am grateful for several chances to work and learn with Coady mentors and colleagues.

I have also really enjoyed co-facilitation with Coady grads who have the same mindset and know what we want to achieve together. It wasn't only delivering the program we had designed earlier, but also helping participants learn how to learn, seeing where they wanted to go and believing that change is possible. I see this as a people-oriented perspective. It is a very rich experience, diverse and integral.

It was a real-life experience to see how different people can complement each other, rather than compete. We trusted in each other's capabilities and we trusted that we, as co-facilitators, would help and learn from each other throughout the process. I call this a safe space of co-facilitation, where you don't feel afraid or worried about making mistakes or missing something. It really added to our enjoyment as co-facilitators when the participants gave us feedback on how we interact and work together. It was a good sign for us that we were doing well.

This was unlike other co-facilitation experiences I have had with people from other backgrounds. In those situations where we had two different paradigms, we only worked on the workshop design, we did not go into how to deliver the deep message of the workshop. Then as co-facilitators, we did not really live the whole transformation experience with the participants. In those situations, I recognized there was a hidden competition among the facilitators! Unintentionally, I found myself uncomfortable, not feeling at ease, judging my co-facilitator; bottom line: it wasn't a safe space to facilitate or learn.

I can assure you that the learning and fun of co-facilitation comes in how we complement each other. It is like a musical orchestra, where each one starts playing her own special instrument with her special style, blending with the others, and it's all OK!

Facilitation Uses Creative Ways such as Graphic Facilitation
Cynthia: The first time I saw and got acquainted with graphic facilitation 'it hooked my heart' and I thought, this is what I want to learn to do. I have an artistic background, love to draw and use colours, and I thought that graphic facilitation was an excellent way to express and visualize ideas, especially for people who are not talkative. I fell in love with the challenge of translating words into simple drawings which reflect and focus on how participants absorb their learning in a workshop.

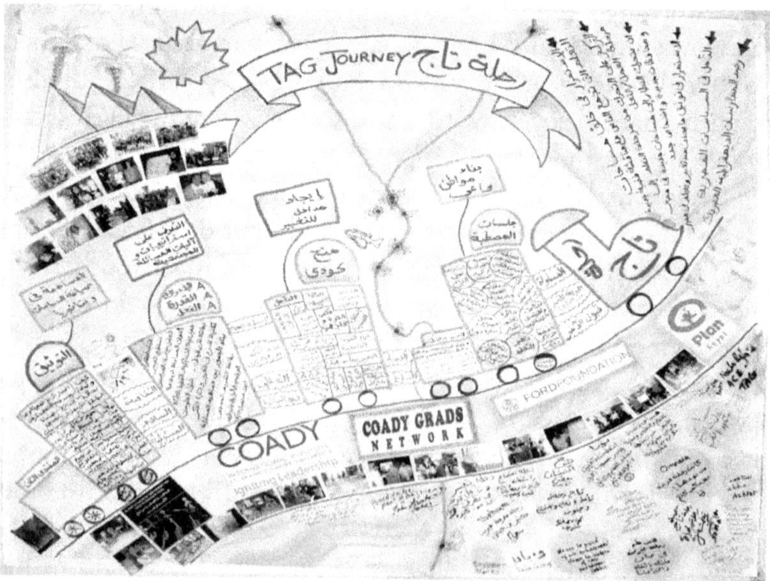

Picture 2: Mural of steps of the TAG project, Egypt.

My first encounter with a real opportunity of being a graphic facilitator was the TAG project (a CGN and Coady partnership focused on Transparency and Accountability in Governance). I was asked to do a mural for the workshop to help reflect on all the steps of the project *(Picture 2)*. I didn't know what to do! "But," I thought, "here in this space, with these people, I can take the challenge because it's ok not to be perfect, and it will be a learning opportunity for me that I don't want to miss." After the four days of the workshop the mural became real, and I would say that I couldn't have done it without the help and inspiration of the whole team. They were very supportive, gave ideas and reflected on the TAG journey, and finally, the TAG train mural became a reality. I made lots of mistakes in this mural but I learned so much more from the experience.

My second big encounter with graphic facilitation was at the Coady where I was co-facilitating a youth course. I thought this is the

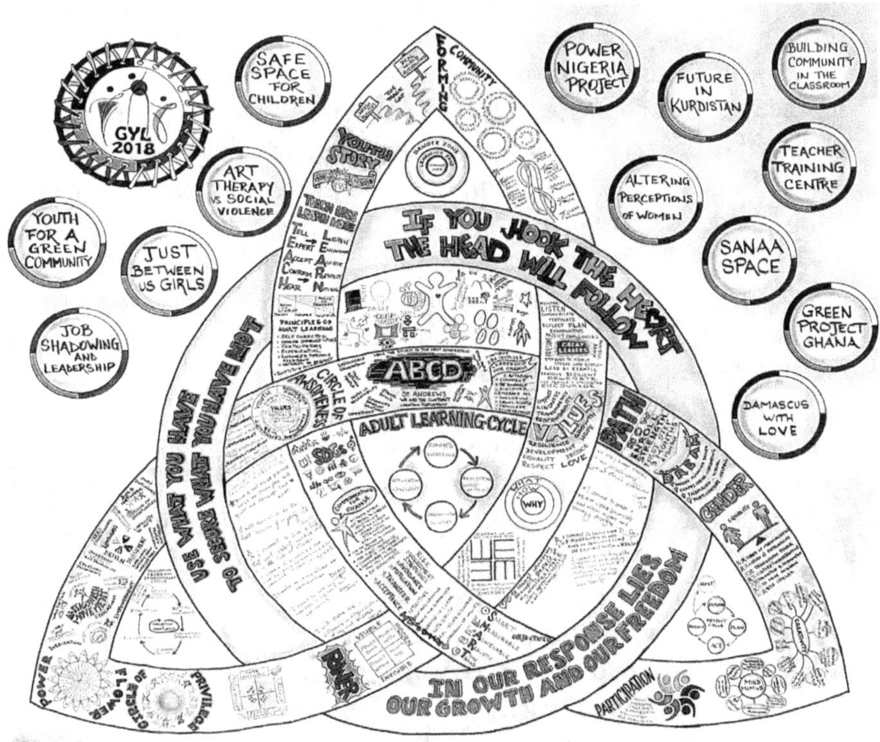

Picture 3: Mural of global youth project learnings.

most inspiring place to start being a real graphic facilitator! I decided to challenge myself, with no idea what I was going to do in the mural that had to be completed within the three weeks of the course! I was very much supported by both my mentor in graphic facilitation and by my co-facilitator *(Picture 3)*. I worked for long hours in designing each part of the mural and I enjoyed staying for hours after participants left the classroom. I'd put on loud music and set about drawing and colouring each part of the mural. I am really happy and thankful I had those great opportunities at the Coady Institute. I have the constant urge to pay back the gift of learning I have received through being a Coady participant and co-facilitator.

Facilitation is Fun in an Enabling Environment

Cynthia: My first course at the Coady was not easy for me as I didn't understand the main content of the course. I had never worked in the content area and I thought I had made the wrong choice! But throughout the three weeks, the enabling, engaging and fun environment made me want to learn more and be part of each and every moment of this course. Actually, I was impressed with the facilitator and the facilitation technique — how it included each of the participants. The tools used were simple yet very interesting and the general atmosphere was very engaging and empowering. There were different levels of knowledge in the classroom which could have put some of us in a corner, not able to participate or be included, but all of us were helped to find our way in. Also, one of the main factors that touched me was the respectful acceptance of the different paces of learning of each participant.

I learned that in an enabling environment, participants are encouraged to take more control of their learning process, while facilitators accept the pace of change happening with each one and address participants equally. Also, the relationship and environment that we, as facilitators, create with participants in the first few hours of a program are very important, as it sets the tone of the whole workshop.

It is like planting different seeds in the same condition. We monitor their development and when it's time, each seed will grow at its own pace and develop in a special way. Some seeds may not grow at all, while others, with plenty of water, will bear fruit. As facilitators, it's our job to create an enabling environment, water the seeds and wait.

Facilitation is Being People-Oriented Inside and Outside the Workshop

Mary: Being at the Coady and observing the facilitators working together, helping and complementing each other was a remarkable experience for me; not only in one course, but in all courses and over several years. The facilitators established a personal relationship with each one of us; they not only listened to our stories, but they cared about it. These relationships continue after the courses have ended. The Coady facilitators connect you with other graduates in your country and they are always there for you when you ask for advice or help. The transformational experience goes beyond the classroom and becomes a long-term relationship. This unique people-oriented relationship was essential as a real transformational experience for me. When I came back to Cairo, I was privileged to work with Coady facilitators and Egyptian Coady graduates and we formed a strong, harmonious facilitators group. We had lots of fun learning together with the participants. When I refer to facilitators, I do not mean only inside the workshops, but in managing long-term projects and the Coady Graduates Network. This experience was evidence for me of the possibility of being a people-oriented facilitator, an efficient manager, an inspirational leader, all while enjoying mutual learning experiences.

My story starts when I thought that I could have the same kind of fun, learning and transformational experience in all workplaces; but as I found out, this was not easy at all.

I was sure from my practical experience that having this utopian environment was possible, but I found I could not transfer or explain it in any of my workplaces. When I tried to explain or even to give a flavour of what this empowering relationship looks like, I would receive messages such as: this is inefficient, unprofessional and not applicable in all workplaces. I believe it is possible and applicable under certain conditions; one of them is to be people-oriented, not object-oriented. These are two competing paradigms. The people-oriented paradigm sees the right people are in the right time and in the right place to learn together. It is a long-term relationship, not time-bound. It believes that all are learning and transforming at different paces and that people themselves are responsible for their learning. It is fun and not a greater workload. It has a road map, but is not a blueprint project. Leadership is important in people-oriented paradigms, whereas hierarchy is at the core in object-oriented paradigms.

I also realized how difficult it is to work with others who have a different mindset from yours. This causes lots of conflict within me. Having said that, it is not impossible to transfer a people-oriented paradigm to your workplace, but it requires lots of self-reflection and awareness, building relationships, doing work differently, and balancing the requirement of managerial requests and above all, patience.

The good news is, after lots of struggle and negotiation, there was success. It is not a personal victory, it is the victory of participation, patience, human relationship and trust. After deep reflection, I realized that people want to see and feel your transformational experience, they want to experience it themselves, not just hear about it, to support you. I also realized that asking for support from like-minded people takes courage, and in order to support each other in providing a living experience, one must never give up. There is always a way.

Smooth Facilitation Requires a Conducive Environment
We have collectively learned that building a conducive environment is a two-fold process; first, there are the relationships and an appreciative atmosphere among participants, and second, there is the infrastructure and the materials used in the facilitation sessions. Both aspects are important to have a transformative experience.

It is important to set a safe space that allows participants and facilitators to share ideas and exchange experiences, information or knowledge in an appreciative and constructive way.

The infrastructure includes the availability of all necessary tools, equipment and materials for facilitation from one side, and a comfortable place for participants on the other.

Once, as facilitators, we found ourselves in a situation where the logistics and the infrastructure for a workshop were not adequate, despite all the preparation and communication before the training. We learned that to overcome these logistical challenges required positive attitudes, tolerance, transparency with the participants, and flexibility from the facilitators. All this helped a lot in building a community of learners. The weakest point in a situation could turn into an opportunity for coming together and working collaboratively. This is easy to say now, but it was hard to remember and follow in the real situation.

These difficult situations that we faced together helped us to be more creative and develop a friendlier and more collaborative learning environment. They also made us laugh as we faced the challenges together, not alone. When such challenges come up in real life, it is an opportunity to show the true spirit of facilitation; sometimes we succeed, sometimes we fail, but there is always a big learning opportunity for us to remember.

Our Learning Continues

When we were invited to contribute to this book by writing about our experience, we chose to write about facilitation and started to share our stories with each other. Some stories brought happy memories and some reminded us of a painful experience. We continued to have reflection sessions to share our stories, analyse them and find similarities and differences. Out of the similarities, we wrote our key learnings and messages. Going through several reflection meetings, we wrote drafts with different styles, using different colours to identify who wrote what. We ended up with this essay where, although we identified individuals, it was everyone's experience and the lessons were applicable to all our individual stories. Writing this essay helped us to overcome painful experiences. In the first draft, we described everything that went wrong in the difficult facilitation experiences. It looked like we had not yet healed from these hard experiences. However, when we got feedback from the editors and stepped out from the details, we were able to draw a bigger picture and find the learning in it. We feel we have healed and have let go of the unpleasant experience, and taken great learning from it.

Out of all our stories we enjoyed sharing during our reflections, we found two key messages we want to highlight in closing:

- We realized that relationships matter in all our actions; through building human relationships, building trust and sharing mutual respect, people can learn and change. No matter what degrees you hold, it matters that you have love for the people you are interacting with.
- In all our stories, we found we all experienced a small activity or an action at the Coady that touched us in one way or another. We found ourselves re-doing it again with others in different contexts

and on a larger scale. There is no better description of the cascading and influencing model than our collective stories.

Finally, we can say our learning journey continues with more awareness and more self-reflection that helps us realize the true meaning of our lives.

Endnotes

1   Senge, P. (1990). The Fifth Discipline: The art and practice of the learning organization. New York, NY: Doubleday/Currency.

2   Kolb, D. (1984). Experiential Learning: Experience as the source of Learning. Hoboken, NJ: Prentice-Hall.

3   Paulo Freire: An incredible conversation. (1996). [video] International Literacy Institute, World Conference on Literacy, Philadelphia, PA. https://www.youtube.com/watch?v=aFWjnkFypFA

4   Steinburg, J. (2014). https://twitter.com/JosephSteinberg/status/462389580625235968

5   Baden-Powell, R.S.S. [n.d.]. https://www.scout.org/node/28744?language=en

High Resolution full colour images of the illustrations in this essay are available on the book's webpage at www.pdltd.net/sprouting-seeds-of-radical-education. Point your smart phone camera at the QR code below to link you directly to the images.

Sixteen

Widening circles of belonging: An essential ingredient towards transformative justice

maureen st. clair, Grenada

"The kind of change we are after is cellular as well as institutional, is personal and intimate, is collective as well as cultural. We are making love synonymous with justice."

Prentis Hemphill [1]

The Grenada Listening Project

What happens when a security guard for the first time leaves his position at the front door; leaves his habitual and customary pose, arms by his side, a hard stare forward (a pose of disconnection and separation) and chooses to join a circle? What happens when a security guard accepts an invitation to place himself inside, not outside a circle? What happens when a security guard chooses a circle with the very youth he is guarding, and with those young men becomes vulnerable, real and relatable?

This is what happens: the security guard shares a story, his story, a story of abuse in the hands of a family member. The youths turn their attention to him. They turn their attention and give presence to a man who normally represents power: a power that punishes not shares. The youths listen to a man standing at that moment on equal ground, a man who is no longer a security guard, but a human with a shared story of violence and trauma. In that moment a brave space becomes braver. In that moment a circle communicates a shared humanity where men old and young listen and witness one another.

Community facilitator, activist and author, adrienne maree brown[2] calls the practice of holding each other in community while critically exploring the root causes of personal and collective trauma, deep healing work and necessary steps towards transformative justice.

The following essay will share stories from the Grenada Listening Project (GLP), a non-profit Grenada-based organization established in 2017 by three Grenadian/Canadian women, myself, Sue Brathwaite and Margot Holas; three women working within the field of mental health, education and community peacebuilding. Three women who share common values and principles grounded in the power of compassionate listening: listening as a form of bearing witness, of widening circles of belonging, of creating paths towards healing personal and collective trauma, and of working collectively towards transformative justice and peace.[3] Included in the essay are quotes from various activists and educators as well as projects from around the world that have inspired us along the way. We appreciate and honour their works in shaping our own.

Into a Circle We Listen
The GLP provides opportunities for people to step into real and metaphorical circles as revealed by the story of the security guard which took place while the GLP worked within a local youth rehabilitation and protection centre. In Grenada, youth are generally considered those under 30 years of age. This was a 12-week program that facilitated a process of building healthy and wise relationships with self and others through community conflict transformative practices. Participants embodied a deeper understanding of violence at a personal, social and systemic level. They engaged in creative practices such as stop action theatre, spoken word poetry, story sharing, writing and exchanging, short films, discussions and a variety of other creative expressions. Security guards and duty officers were invited into these facilitated spaces to do the work with the youth.

Another example of folks stepping into listening/witnessing/belonging circles involved a session with youth at a local skills training school. Allison Harris, a youth facilitator (trained in conflict transformation/compassionate listening) and I created an intentional space for youth to be heard, seen, acknowledged and witnessed while engaged in various participatory activities that allowed them to think critically and creatively related to conflicts they were experiencing.

I remember in one of the sessions, the slow quiet voice of a youth grumbling his feelings into the circle: "I feel to take my pencil and juke the eye of he over there," his chin pointing to another young man. Allison reflected back his feeling of anger: "You vex?" The young man glaring in front of him nodded yes. Allison asked where he felt the vexation in his body and the youth took time to locate the anger before saying, "All over." Allison thanked him for speaking up, expressing and feeling. Allison commented that the first step in making a conscious response to anger was listening to our bodies, emotions and thoughts. She shared with the students that once we can pause, notice and locate the heightened emotions in our bodies and name the emotion, we are then in a better position to make a choice between actually picking up a pencil or cutlass and juking or chopping someone or not. I witnessed the same youth's shoulders drop from his ears. I saw him loosen his folded arms. I saw how he lifted his gaze and glanced at Allison. I saw Allison position her body giving this youth her full presence.

Allison and I came to this particular session knowing about a fight the night before down on the old airport road that resulted in one youth dead from a cutlass wound and the other youth in jail. In the circle we learned both men in the violent conflict were friends with a few youths in the circle, and in particular, the man who confessed his rage minutes before.

Other students slowly began to express themselves as Allison and I reflected back some of the facts, feelings and values they were expressing. We also offered deepening questions such as "What do you believe caused such a violent response to this conflict?" and "Where do you find the strength and courage to deal with the loss of friends and family?" This allowed the youth to go deeper into their analysis of the fatal conflict and deeper into their own grieving process. Their contributions to the root causes of the violence were reflected back and written on a flipchart. Examples included power, shame and masculine stereotypes. We also spent time documenting their responses to finding strength and courage as they moved through their grief. Examples included music, prayer, family and football. We believe the youth were able to access their own shared knowledge and experiences. Doing this builds their capacity to hold complex stories and witness each other. They also bear witness to the violent, unjust systems where many youths' lives are violently ruptured, sometimes irreparably. The youth are also able to access their inner capacity to hold and process grief by identifying their personal strengths and actions that can help them move forward.

One of the teachers afterward commented she had never experienced the men open up in the class before. Allison responded by saying she believed once brave spaces were built, where people felt heard and acknowledged, then people will share and listen. The GLP believe this is an example of alternative ways to address and interrupt violence, which do not rely on the punitive justice systems of the state, but on the wisdom, intuition and love of human beings building brave spaces and bridges back to one another.

Embodying Radical Empathy on Streets, Parks and within Local Institutes

In 2017, a compassionate listening workshop was held in preparation for the Global Free Listening Movement, a movement born in the streets of Los Angeles, where people determined to challenge the status quo took to the streets to listen, hear and acknowledge people's concerns, experiences, knowledge and emotions. The GLP took to the streets, parks and blocks for the next three years. The GLP trained folks in compassionate listening. We aligned ourselves within those trainings and with active definitions of compassion, such as those of Buddhist teacher Pema Chödrön, who believes compassion is knowing our darkness well enough so we can show up without judgment in other people's darkness.[4] Bishop Desmond Tutu clarifies that compassion is not merely sentimental, but demanding and action oriented.[5]

In our debriefing circles we shared similar experiences and reflections of building our muscle for presence and compassion. The GLP agrees with activist, writer and Buddhist teacher reverend angel Kyodo williams when she states, "Presence allows us to see ourselves and others. By choosing presence we learn to let go of our own discomfort, experience ourselves in a trusting way, allowing us to trust others more, and as a result we are drawn deeper."[6]

The GLP is also in alliance with David Augsburger's words: "Being heard is so close to being loved that for the average person, they are almost indistinguishable."[7] The GLP believes we must begin nothing less than a revolution of the heart; nothing less than standing in our shared humanity, in order to come together and recognize the violent systems dividing and disconnecting people and communities; recognizing the need to re-imagine and co-create systems similar to what we are creating in alternative spaces of compassion, presence and love.

The Director of Human Rights Grenada, Milton Coy, shared a touching story from his time as a Free Listener at a local mental health institute. This story was the impetus for the GLP's workshop called Sharing Stories, Embodying Empathy and Building Community. The story was about a man who came into the lobby of a mental health institute flanked by two police officers. The man looked at Milton and motioned with his eyes to Milton's Free Listening sign. Milton asked the officers if he could listen to the prisoner. The officers said, "No." The prisoner and Milton's eyes met, and Milton 'presenced' himself by standing close and holding this man's attention with his own attention. Milton expressed a deep sense of connection. Later, when Milton revealed the man's identity and showed empathy for this man, we were shocked. Almost 10 years ago this same man committed a horrendous crime murdering his two friends in a psychotic fit. He was labeled a monster, a demon; understandably there was not much compassion nationally in wanting to understand this man's story. We witnessed Milton swell with compassion and thus humanize this man who committed such a violent crime. Even without a known story, we felt a shared and tragic humanness with this individual through Milton as he held the imagined complexities of this man's story without judgment, interpretation or blame, enabling us to do the same.

The collective experience of compassion ignited by Milton's sharing, as well as by the work of Narrative 4, a global network of educators, students and artists, was inspiring. They use art and storytelling to build empathy between people and communities while equipping them to improve their communities and the world. We hosted two additional workshops. People came together to learn compassionate listening skills while sharing stories of struggles within their own lives. They exchanged their stories with another person and had the opportunity to walk in the hearts and minds of another, while also witnessing their stories re-told in first person by another. People exchanged stories with people who held various identities and thus took on the other's stories, whether it was an exchange of genders, cultures, class, age, mental health or race. Participants commented how powerful it was to become someone else's story of struggle, and how for some there were shifts of consciousness related to curiosity vs judgment, connection vs separation, and love vs indifference.

The GLP also facilitated a series of workshops with a secondary school drama group based on the work of Augusto Boal, Brazilian popular educator and founder of Theatre of the Oppressed.[8] Students learned compassionate listening skills while sharing stories of youth-centered community based conflict in small groups. In these groups they chose one story and re-enacted the conflict. With the help of a facilitator and the audience they were able to try out creative ways of interrupting and possibly transforming the conflict by acting out different nonviolent possibilities. The groups chose conflicts related to LGBTQI+ issues, gender-based violence, teacher and student conflicts, and child abuse. By embodying the various roles of characters, their struggles and possible new ways of responding/changing/ hearing various perspectives, students and teachers collaborated in co-imagining and co-creating alternative paths to the violence that erupted in the various enactments of the conflict. In the larger debriefing circles students and teachers had the opportunity to equalize the space and share their opinions, reflections and learnings. We heard teachers express surprise about how open and responsive students were, especially students they don't usually hear from, and in particular male students. Again, we were able to acknowledge the power of brave space where people felt heard, seen and validated, thus enabling all voices to find a sense of belonging and the courage to be vulnerable and share their experiences and opinions.

Weekly Online Listening Circles and Conflict Transformation Trainings

The GLP was getting ready to host two programs before the COVID-19 pandemic hit, one at Grenada's National College and one at the prison. Listening benches were built. These were inspired by Zimbabwe's Friendship Benches, a community program intervention providing safe spaces and a sense of belonging for folks suffering with anxiety and depression. Compassionate Listening trainings were organized, inspired by The Compassionate Listening Project, a not-for-profit organization that grew out of reconciliation work in Israel and Palestine. All these were set up for teachers, students, prison staff and inmates. The trainings were to help people manage, facilitate and provide opportunities where people could be heard, seen and acknowledged in whatever struggles they were experiencing.

Unfortunately, the programs did not transpire, but instead online weekly listening circles were implemented, enabling people to join online spaces where people could share stories of struggle and stories of hope while learning and practicing compassionate listening skills. We also provided back-to-back international online trainings in conflict transformation and compassionate listening, where more than 40 participants (the majority from Grenada) were trained in various conflict transformation skills, tools and practices using compassionate listening as the foundation. Participants shared similar feedback related to learning what it means to fully embrace our humanness through modelling what it means to be human on a basic level, through listening and sharing from the heart. This recalls adrienne maree brown words, "simply being present to each other is our most basic moral obligation."[9]

Closing Circle

In Angie and John Paul Lederach's book When Blood and Bones Cry Out, Judy Atkinson writes:

> "Only we can raise our individual voices to make a collective song of healing. Only we can choose to sit in circles and listen and learn together. Only we can put into action what we have learned, knowing that as we nurture spaces for healing and reconciliation, we do so from our own experiences and a longing for a renewed world, in which humans live and work together with mutual care and respect for each other and the lifeworld in which we all live."[10]

The GLP believes teaching the skills and tools to build and enhance people's capacity to listen helps people connect deeply with themselves, with each other and the natural world — the foundation to reclaiming and repairing the human spirit which reverend angel Kyodo williams states is essential in working towards justice. "Imagining anything different," williams says, "is to have our heads buried in the sand of hundreds of years of domination, colonization that every one of us is colluding with and participating in consciously and unconsciously."[11]

The GLP is grounded within the consciousness of a shared human history of trauma, and thus believes personal and collective trauma has the power to unite, repair, reclaim and widen circles of belonging.

The GLP cultivates deep rooted listening for hearing and witnessing the multiple contexts of people's stories, that is, the systems and structures that hold up, and/or violently restrict individuals, families, workplaces and communities. The GLP believes by listening and bearing witness collectively we dive deeper into a critical analysis and thus a collective understanding of how the violence/harm/trauma manifests itself, lodges itself inside individual bodies, communities and institutes. We believe the work of listening and hearing one another's personal and collective stories on multiple levels is the foundation to becoming collaborators in co-imagining, and co-creating a more just, equitable and compassionate world.

What a deep honour to work, live, breathe the works of the GLP. I have stretched, grown and deepened my understanding of what it means to embody conflict from a generative and transformative perspective; what it means to bring our full exquisite, complex humanness to courageous spaces to see, feel, hear and witness one another as a means of nourishing our shared human need: belonging and connection. A deep bow of gratitude for all of us who circled over the past days, months and years; may we continue the work of self and community healing, one circle at a time!

Endnotes

1   Hemphill, P. https://prentishemphill.com/homepage

2   brown, a. m. (2017). Emergent Strategy: Shaping change, changing worlds. Chico, CA: AK Press, p. 135.

3   Websites foundational to the work of the GLP:

Narrative 4: https://narrative4.com/

Compassionate Listening Project:
https://www.compassionatelistening.org/

Zimbabwe Friendship Benches:
www.friendshipbenchzimbabwe.org

4   Chödrön, P. (2001.) The Places that Scare You: A guide to fearlessness in difficult times. Boulder, CO: Shambhala Publications.

5   Tutu, D. [n.d.]. AZ QUOTES:
https://www.azquotes.com/quote/555933

6   williams, a.K., Owens, L.R., & Syedullah, J. (2016). Radical Dharma: Talking race, love and liberation. Berkeley, CA: North Atlantic Books, p. 98.

7   Augsburger, D. (1982). BrainyQuote:
https://www.brainyquote.com/quotes/david_augsburger_627321

8   A description of Theatre of the Oppressed can be found on the website Acting Now:
http://actingnow.co.uk/what-is-theatre-of-the-oppressed/

9   brown, a. m., (2017). Emergent Strategy: Shaping change, changing worlds. Chico, CA: AK Press, p. 88.

10 Atkinson, J., in Lederach, J.P. & Lederach, A.J. (2010). When Blood and Bones Cry Out: Journeys through the soundscape of healing and reconciliation. New York, NY: Oxford University Press, [foreword, p. xiv].

11 williams, a.K., Owens, L.R., & Syedullah, J. (2016). Radical Dharma: Talking race, love and liberation. Berkeley, CA: North Atlantic Books, p. 99.

Seventeen

Spiritual reflections on bullying and forgiveness

Susan MacKay, Canada

"Dangerous memories have two dimensions: that of hope and that of suffering."[1]

Sharon Welch

During one of my Master of Adult Education graduate classes, the professor created a series of exquisitely hand-painted bookmarks, each with a quotation, and kindly gifted one to each student. As I read the serendipitous quote on the bookmark I had randomly received, it struck my heart, starkly reminding me of the seemingly hopeless crossroads at which I found myself outside the safety of this learning environment — at the juncture between "that of hope and that of suffering."

Similar to masking the internal emotional and physiological reaction I was experiencing in the classroom, I was trying to conceal a real-life bullying experience in the workplace. Despite my ongoing efforts to endure, minimize, excuse, ignore, deny and sometimes even attempt to rationalize or justify the bullying behaviours, none of these responses rectified a progressively unbearable, worsening situation and its debilitating physical, mental and psychological effects, personally and professionally.

As a person who searches for meaningful moments and spiritual significance in my life, receiving this bookmark was a transformative critical incident or "disorienting dilemma."[2] It posed an immediate, definitive question about which academic and spiritual path I would choose at this juncture in my life. The decision of what to do with the "dangerous memories" of my bullying experience weighed heavily on my heart — the unknown and the in between can be distressing places.

The decisive response to my bullying quandary was a convergence of the application of transformative learning, critical theory, emancipatory education, Freirean pedagogy, power, the beautiful bookmark, and a second piece of written artistic expression, the philosophical lyrics of a song.

Derived from the Ancient Greek word kritikós, the etymological meaning of "critical" is judgment or discernment. The more I delved into the essence of critical theory and the emancipatory pedagogy of Brazilian educator Paulo Freire, the more I began to critically reflect upon and apply *conscientização* (conscientization), a concept in Freire's seminal work Pedagogy of the Oppressed,[3] to my experience. I would listen to The Pass, a song written by the late brilliant Neil Peart, lyricist and drummer for the Canadian band Rush. The lyrics seemed to embody where I was situated at The Pass: perpetually faced with a barricade of disempowerment — ceaseless scrutiny, humiliating subjugation, enduring criticism and voiceless silencing — or the possibility of empowerment and realization that "it's not as if this barricade blocks the only road, it's not as if [I'm] all alone." Peart's lyrics spoke to my heart: no longer would I remain "lost in the darkness…straining at invisible chains…trembling on that rocky ledge." And I would not lose "the will to fight."[4] By engaging in critical reflection, I made a conscious choice to find meaning in my oppressive experience; I would use the emancipatory power of education as a means of empowerment to create awareness about workplace bullying and prevent bullying from happening to other people. But, in order to educate others, I had to first educate myself by conducting research about the phenomenon of workplace bullying and the concept of power.

A quote in Critical Pedagogy: Notes from the Real World intrigued my curiosity about power and powerlessness: "Unless we ourselves are empowered, we cannot be involved with any other process of empowerment. To be voiceless is to be powerless."[5] Throughout my graduate degree, I sought to understand the concepts of power and powerlessness — how they are applied, exercised and exploited; and what it is to be powerless, disempowered, silenced versus powerful, empowered, vocal (using one's voice).

The notion of power had always held a negative connotation for me, especially within a bullying context where power was exerted over me. A form of psychological violence, bullying is the abuse of power: the deliberate destructive disempowerment of targets/victims. The late anti-workplace bullying campaigner Tim Field defines workplace bullying as:

> "Bullying is not tough management. Its purpose is to hide inadequacy and [it is] a form of thuggery which prevents people from doing their job. Where bullying exists [you will] find disenchantment, demotivation, demoralization, disenfranchisement, disempowerment, disloyalty, disaffection, dysfunction, inefficiency, cynicism, alienation and an 'us-and-them' culture, constant conflict, an unpleasant atmosphere, misery, unhappy staff, a climate of fear, high staff turnover, high sickness absence, low productivity, impaired performance, stifled creativity, low morale, zero team spirit, poor customer service, and mistakes in delivery of products and services. The cost of these is rarely accounted."[6]

For their own survival in a hostile workplace, targets/victims often choose to remain silent and work even harder, leading to burnout and exhaustion. The attempt to meet unattainable expectations — often with the intent of setting one up for failure — reinforces the cycle of helplessness, hopelessness and admonishment through the use of 'power over.' The impact of bullying behaviours (note I do not refer to people as "bullies") affects targets/victims in a myriad of ways: physically and physiologically (health), psychologically (emotional and mental), and financially (being forced to quit one's job is "the ultimate level of silencing.")[7] As is evidenced in bullying literature, some targets/victims of bullying endure post-traumatic stress disorder (PTSD) symptoms years after their demeaning experience has ended.

In contrast to my personal understanding about power over, the most important aspect of learning about power was gaining the knowledge, insight and affirmation that each of us possesses 'power within.' We are empowered by our own voice and our own agency; how we choose to wield our personal power either empowers or disempowers others.

Since my academic and professional goals were to provide education about the facets of workplace bullying, I applied to a provincial union that was in the process of hiring anti-bullying workplace facilitators and was accepted into the program. I served in this role for five years. Although I was immensely looking forward to meeting my peers at the upcoming training session, I felt quite anxious — would

I have to speak about my personal experience with workplace bullying? I hoped not. This was in my past, right? I just wanted to move
forward on my educational path.

Throughout the training session, I still felt quite fragile and looking back at this time in my life, I would describe myself as "smarting"
— I was unwilling and unable to speak about my experience. It was
too painful and nothing about these "dangerous memories" made any
sense. What I did not understand was that liberating myself emotionally and spiritually meant having an honest conversation with myself
to try and somehow reconcile what had happened, to begin to heal.

At the end of the session, each facilitator was invited to voluntarily
share their thoughts. I was not planning to say anything but when it
was my turn I did speak. I began to candidly articulate my experience
with bullying and the more details I disclosed, the stronger and more
empowered I felt. By applying Freirean pedagogy to my experience, I
named 'it' and I was no longer voiceless.

A few days after the training, I received an unexpected email
from one of the facilitators, titled "Go Girl," which encapsulates the
moment I spoke:

> "I wanted to send a quick note and say that it felt right to
> hear you express what you expressed today. It seemed to
> me like watching a type of empowerment/freedom happen-
> ing in real-time. When you have something like that
> happen before your eyes, you only to want to validate and
> encourage it; so, I'm sending this message to do just that.
>
> I could recognize what was happening within you
> because it goes to the core of our humanity. The
> long-standing oppression that you described and the
> transformation that accompanied seeing and reflecting
> this - from your inner world to your outer world (us in
> that moment); and you're right, we know this experience
> instinctively to be: real...true...liberating...transforma-
> tive...re-empowering (I believe it's important to point to,
> acknowledge and to honour such a moment in time)."

In vocalizing my experience, I was no longer silenced, "straining at invisible chains… trembling on that rocky ledge." Speaking
honestly about "dangerous memories" of being bullied, without fear
or embarrassment in a safe, supportive learning environment was a

transformational, hopeful moment in my healing journey. Except for my loved ones, closest friends and a few colleagues, I had not shared my experience, which was laden with intimate feelings of suffering, sadness and shame. I still had not reconciled my "dangerous memories" on a personal level; I left them compartmentalized in the past where I did not have to think about them.

As I determinedly fulfilled the requirements for my graduate degree while serving as an anti-bullying facilitator, I developed many adult education workshops whose foci ranged from employment related conflict resolution and team building to Laughter Yoga (peacebuilding). As I was constantly learning from co-facilitators and workshop participants, facilitating workshops was a meaningful and edifying educational experience.

The concept of self-reflection is an essential component of adult education. As I engaged in ongoing critical and reflective analysis of my growth and practice as a facilitator, it became apparent I was at another reflective crossroads about my authenticity as an adult educator. As I continued to facilitate sessions about power over and power within, the lingering "dangerous memories" of anguish, loss and grief and their subsequent costly consequences to my life remained.

Engaging in self-criticism and self-reflection presented me with the opportunity to carefully consider and evaluate who I was and aspired to be as an adult educator, and what it was to speak and teach with an authentic voice. If I were to continue facilitating workshops, would I not have to embody and emulate peace? How could I educate others about emancipatory education if I was still emotionally "straining at invisible chains?" While I taught about peacebuilding, could I speak with integrity if I carried anger and resentment, the antithesis of peace and forgiveness? And what is it to teach peace with authenticity if you know, in your own heart, you have none? Even if no one else was aware, I knew.

Once again, I spent contemplative time discerning in prayer, mindful meditation and journal writing as I sought to resolve the conundrum of transcendence from the "dangerous memories". Thus far on my adult education path, I had learned to understand aspects of power through the engagement of critical analysis, self-reflection and meaning making. From an educational perspective, I had methodically dealt with bullying. It was time to discover the spiritual significance and transformational potential in this experience and to rediscover joy in my life.

Throughout my enduring quest for internal peace, a figurative Laughing Buddha had quietly and serendipitously been hanging on our living room wall all this time, with this quote: "Let us discover the significance of birth and the joy of living."

When the Student is Ready, the Teacher will Appear

Many years ago, after a visit to Higashi-Honganji Temple in Kyoto, the ancient capital of Japan, I showed my dear friend and *shodō* (Japanese calligraphy) teacher a photo I had taken of a quote located on the side of a Buddhist temple. My friend quietly observed the joy I described in discovering this spiritual blessing and unbeknownst to me, she created an elegant piece of calligraphy as a parting gift when I left Japan at the end of my teaching contract.

Since my visit to this temple, the notion of discovering my "significance of birth and the joy of living" has guided me in contemplating life's meaning and its purpose. A lifelong learner, I tend to perceive life experiences as having educational and spiritual value. I envisage the potential learning in all situations, no matter how challenging or seemingly negative, as opportunities for personal and spiritual growth.

In trying to reconcile the bullying experience, I sought to rediscover the "significance of birth" and "the joy of living." This meant accepting what had happened, finding meaning in the experience and moving forward on a transcendent path of compassion and forgiveness with purposeful peace.

As there was a choice in the decision to bully me by exerting power over, I too, had a choice in my decision to exercise power within; I chose the path of forgiveness. In prayerful meditation, I blessed, released and forgave the bullying experience, "[Remembering] that forgiveness too is a power. To beg for it is a power, and to withhold or bestow it is a power, perhaps the greatest."[8]

After my prayer of forgiveness, below is an excerpt of what I wrote in my journal:

> I will make this experience educational, make it spiritual,
> make it meaningful.
> I will educate and empower.

I will speak. And help others find their voice. And speak
for the voiceless.
I choose love. I choose light. I choose hope.

No longer being defined by a bullying experience and choosing
hope meant rediscovering "the joy of living" by transcending nega-
tivity and embracing elements of joy. As a certified Laughter Yoga
instructor, I incorporated elements of my training into my personal
spiritual practice using humour to promote psychological and physiological health and wellness. This type of playful yoga is transformative
in its capacity to heal through creativity, imagination and spontaneity.
Any participant can be a lantern of hope illuminating the importance
of play through the discovery of their authentic voice and truth, and
in their ability to peacefully transcend and heal from difficult experiences.[9] There is much joy and liberation in "Ho Ho Ha Ha Ha"-ing!

For the next few years, I continued to passionately facilitate
anti-bullying workshops and co-organized two Pink Shirt Days
to raise awareness about creating bully-free environments and the
power of kindness; after all, bullying and kindness cannot co-exist.
The theme of Pink Shirt Day 2014 was: Wear Pink - Be Kind - Be
the Change. Wearing pink and being kind are steps toward taking a
collective stand against bullying and changing our culture to create
bully-free schools, communities and workplaces. Everyone has a role
to play in eliminating bullying in our schools, workplaces, society and
creating a culture of civility, equality, dignity and respect.

After I graduated with my Master of Adult Education degree,
I amalgamated my passion for adult education and community
development and my experience with facilitation and program
planning to develop my own program: *The PATH — (Positive,
Appreciative, Teamwork, Holistic) to Workplace Wellness* for adult learners. Throughout the PATH emphasis is placed on the correlation of
individual and collective communication and language (language
is action), the relational aspects of power, and how each affects and
determines the health and well-being of workplace cultures.

My story illustrates the power of our language and words in
their constructive or destructive capacity: to empower or to disempower; to heal or to hurt; or to create "dangerous memories of hope
and of suffering." Since the inception of my adult education career,

words have influenced my educational, academic and spiritual path — whether it be a gifted bookmark with a serendipitous quote, the philosophical lyrics of a rock song, a Portuguese word embodying the concept of critically awakening, an email honouring the empowering moment of reclaiming my voice, a sacred Buddhist teaching, healing through yogic breathing and syllabic chanting, or an excerpt from feminist dystopian literature. Within each experience, words had the cathartic, transformational power to ignite and foster meaningful change: finding my voice through the recognition of power within.

As adult educators, we must engage in the educational practice of freedom[10] and speak truth to power by courageously and determinedly speaking out against and denouncing all forms of oppression and injustice. Collectively, we must break cultures of silence by giving voice to the voiceless and helping others to speak. Even though finding your voice can be a daunting process, we all have the right to find it.[11]

In the spirit of hope, let us commit to cultivating communities of kindness and compassion — by empowering all members of society to "discover [their] significance of birth and [their] joy of living" so they might live in the words of the Reverend Dr. Moses Coady — "a full and abundant life."

Endnotes

1   Welch, S.D. (2017). Communities of Resistance and Solidarity: A feminist theology of liberation. Eugene, OR: Wipf and Stock Publishers, p. 36.

2   Mezirow, J. (1997). Transformative theory out of context. Adult Education Quarterly, Vol. 48, no. 1, p. 60.

3   Freire, P. (1993) Pedagogy of the Oppressed. (revised ed.) New York, NY: Continuum International Publishing.

4   Rush. (1989). The Pass [song lyrics]: https://www.rush.com/songs/the-pass/

5   Wink, J. (2005). Critical Pedagogy: Notes from the real world. (3rd ed.) New York, NY: Pearson Education, p. 3.

6   Field, T. (2002) as cited in Turney, L. (2003). Mental health and workplace bullying: The role of power, professions and 'on the job' training. Australian e-Journal for the Advancement of Mental Health (AeJAMH). Vol. 2, no. 2, p. 2.

7   Lutgen-Sandvik, P. (2006) as cited in Sobre-Denton, M. S. (2012). Stories from the cage: Autoethnographic sensemaking of workplace bullying, gender discrimination and white privilege. Journal of Contemporary Ethnography. Vol. 41, no. 2, p. 228.

8   Atwood, M. (1985). The Handmaid's Tale. Toronto, ON: McClelland & Stewart, p. 156.

9   St. Thomas, B. & Johnson, P. (2004). Play: The lantern of hope. Journal of Poetry Therapy. Vol. 17, no. 2, pp. 81-90.

10 Freire, P. (1976). Education: The practice of freedom. London, UK: Writers and Readers Publishing Cooperative.

11 Rodenburg, P. (1992). The Right to Speak: Working with the voice. London, UK: Methuen.

— Eighteen —

Virtual global networking during the COVID-19 pandemic

Darren C Brown, Canada and Dániel Törő, Hungary

Organizational colleagues and development practitioners convening in the Zoom Room and Microsoft Teams during the 2020 phase of the COVID-19 pandemic were initially skeptical. Surprisingly they bloomed with successful enthusiasm. As 2020 fatigued, however, so too did the zoomish energy! Without doubt, the experiments with online and virtual platforms demonstrated both significant successes as well as tiresome failures. Migrating previous workshop-styled trainings online was doable, but they were certainly not life giving nor inspirational. However, with thoughtful dialogue design and appropriate use of technology, a portal for strengthening global learning networks magically opened.

The first half of this essay highlights insights and tips for innovating with virtual networking and dialogue to strengthen learning and change. The insights are drawn from reflections on three interventions:

- three 2020 United Nations Food and Agricultural Organization FIRST learning and change initiatives to strengthen teams and global networks;
- an international NGO learning inquiry conducted with young women leaders and mentors in East Africa and Southeast Asia; and,
- migrating previously developed training sessions to the virtual space on behalf of various government agencies.

The tips are entirely functional in nature, referring to the how-to of designing and facilitating virtual and online learning.

We anticipate continuing to facilitate global dialogues, strengthening networks and building movements in 2021 and beyond. Firstly, because we expect continued lockdowns, restrictions on travel and face-to-face convening due to the pandemic, but also, more importantly, because we have experienced unique and meaningful learning results, with considerably fewer resources and a far smaller carbon footprint than traditional face-to-face workshops. We are excited for 'What now?' and in the second part of this essay we share several unresolved challenges and possible considerations to advance global and collective learning and change.

Inspirations

Here are 10 inspirations, highlights and tips to strengthen virtual global networking and dialogue for learning and change from our own practice and reflections over the past year.

Partner with a Champion who Values Learning and Risk-taking: Designing for and facilitating dialogue and learning in the virtual space demands an appetite for risk. Practice has shown that involving a diversity of team members and participants in the design thinking phase of the initiative is a wise risk mitigation response.

Verbal and nonverbal communication work differently in the virtual space than in face-to-face meetings or workshop encounters. Based on the visual real time component, the mind can be tricked into thinking we are together, but in fact we are not. There are multiple distractions that can easily get in the way of clear communication. Mistakes and misunderstandings will occur. Playfulness is key. The success of the initiative is highly dependent on how the leadership shows up. Commitment to learning is the essential ingredient to success.

Design a Learning Pathway with an Eye to Timing rather than Time: Imagine designing a one, two or even three-day workshop, but spreading it over two, four or six weeks — there is the powerful potential inherent in focusing on timing a series of focused learning interventions, rather than designing for one singularly extended time. Conventional workshops demand that participants show up together in one geographical place at one time. To keep things cost and resource efficient, agendas are often tightly scripted leaving little time for quiet reflection and individual sense making. In the virtual space, participants can convene anytime and from anywhere with adequate internet access. This allows for 90-120 minute cascading or sequential sessions scheduled over a period of time, thus enabling meaningful reflection for the participants and thoughtful iterative design by facilitators. This design approach, quite different than the workshop, has been called a learning pathway. This approach leverages the luxury of thoughtful pacing and timing, rather than being stressed out over the time crunch. Micro-Biome: The Missing Link? *(Picture 1)* is an illustrative example of learning pathway design thinking, six sessions over one month.

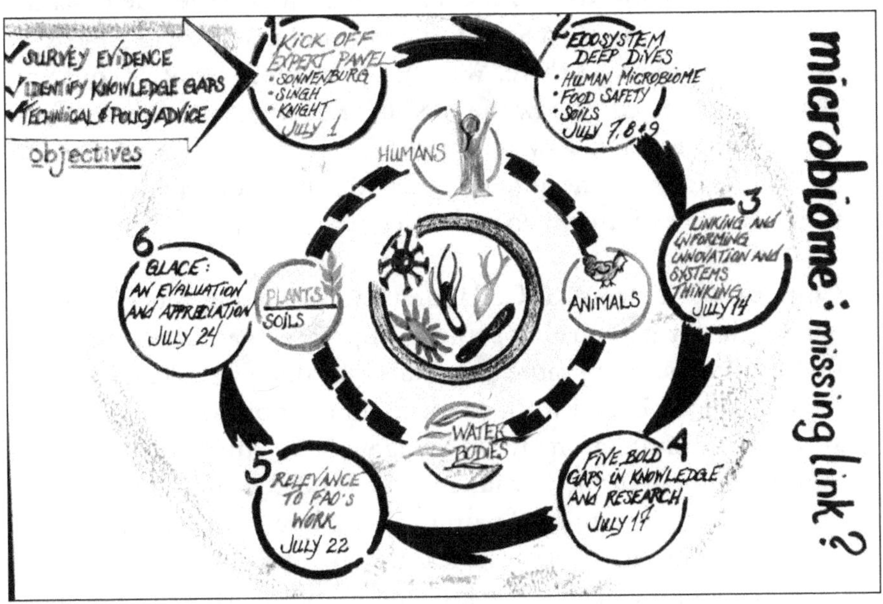

Picture 1: Illustration of the timing of a learning pathway.

Design for Synchronous, Asynchronous and Back Channel Modalities: The synchronous space, real time and face-to-face, is demanding and taxing on the eyes and body. Use the synchronous time wisely and engage participants in meaningful dialogue. No more than two or three open-ended questions of inquiry are required. Play between sufficient small group discussions (three participants per group is optimal) and plenary sense making to build a shared vision. The asynchronous space can be used to archive relevant learning material: articles, PPT presentations, videos, etc. which participants can view at their convenience. Create a forum or a discussion thread in the asynchronous platform to maintain and enhance the collaborative learning spirit. The back channel is a modality for quick announcements to the participant group or messaging between facilitators when the learning initiative is live. The most effective back channel for us has proven to be WhatsApp. Finally, calling upon the agility of participants with technology, use the asynchronous platform and back channel functions during the synchronous session to build up the comfort and attention of participants.

Set Learning Objectives and Complement with a Detailed Dialogue Design: Know where you want to arrive and map a dialogue-based learning design to get there. What is the learning result or concrete change anticipated? Draw upon Kolb's Experiential Learning Cycle[1] to inform the design flow and methods of the learning pathway. As dialogue is key and meaningful reflection time honoured, be open to the emergence of unanticipated outcomes.

Co-Create Principles for Collaborative Learning in the Virtual Space: The virtual learning pathway approach enables meaningful learning, but even more importantly, if done well, lends itself to building a learning network or community of practice. Key to this is keeping in mind that many are living with the stress of COVID-19 lockdowns, quarantines, or illness. The gendered and intercultural influences and dynamics of working from home will also influence participation. Launch the learning pathway by co-creating a set of principles for collaborative learning in the virtual space during COVID-19. This might be as simple as asking the question, "For this space and time to be an accessible, meaningful, and inclusive learning environment and experience for you, what qualities or ways of being would you hope to experience?" Explore mutually shared learning curiosities amongst participants to build shared commitment to co-journeying along the learning pathway.

Walk the Talk of Social Inclusion and Accessibility: Prior to launching the learning pathway, introduce the virtual learning technology to ensure accessibility and tech check the online tools with participants. Offer mini tutorials and coach participants encouragingly. Start on time and stick to agreed limits of synchronous time. Open the synchronous space 15-30 minutes early and invite participants to enter the space for informal social exchanges. End on the agreed time by offering each participant a chance to close with a word or sentence of appreciation or learning.

Seize the Opportunity for Intergenerational Co-facilitation, Co-learning and Co-mentoring: An unanticipated intergenerational learning opportunity can open whilst shifting collaborative convenings to the virtual space. Getting learning pathways right requires a balance between the agility required to effectively navigate the virtual technology, and experience in designing and facilitating dialogue for learning and change. Recognize and value the fact that Millennials often have the lifetime experience and muscle memory to swiftly set up and facilitate in the virtual space. This is balanced with the technical expertise of a senior facilitator skilled in designing participatory dialogues for learning and change. No amount of structured coaching could equate with the mutually valuable learning and relationship building inherent in this co-learning and co-facilitating opportunity. Furthermore, the intergenerational insights shared from hope-based foresight and experience-based hindsight are co-supportive to navigating the territory of a global pandemic.

Monitor Participation and Learning to Maintain the Iterative Richness of the Learning Pathway: There are numerous techniques for assessing participation and learning during the pathway initiative. It can happen informally and live in the synchronous space, or be more deliberately structured and offered in the asynchronous space where participants can respond in anonymity.

Given the learning pathway approach of stretching and sequencing a series of appropriately designed short learning interventions over an extended period of time, facilitators might also consider opening and sharing the process of monitoring learning, collecting evaluative feedback and co-facilitation with participants. Equally important is that co-facilitators lead check-ins on a regular basis to assess their own observations, insights and suggested adaptations.

Incorporate Visual Learning Pathway as Maps and Graphic Trajectories: The learning pathway is designed to be implemented and mapped over a specific period of time. Illustrating the pathway graphically, introducing it at the launch of the learning pathway initiative, and using it to open each successive session thereafter strengthens a shared understanding of the co-learning journey. A singular graphic holds the holism of the learning pathway. A graphic from Young Women Leadership and Mentoring Initiative: A Learning Inquiry captured and held the intention and focus of an eight-month co-learning process *(Picture 2)*.

Picture 2: One graphic can capture the learning pathway.

Laugh – Laugh a Lot at Yourself and with Others: We are living amidst a global pandemic, an unprecedented time for all of us, as we try new ways of learning to work for social transformation and equitable change in the virtual space. Really, it is all a bit surreal. Along the co-learning journey, laughter will serve us all. Take the time to laugh. Loudly!

Challenges and Bottlenecks
We also reflected on challenges and bottlenecks we continue to
encounter and the ideas we have in moving forward as we ask, "What
now? Where next?"

Maintaining Learning Momentum in the Network: As with many
traditional workshops/network events, we often lose the momentum to engage participants beyond the learning event. There is no
follow-up on the learning, or in other words, the application of the
learning, and strengthening relationships is not part of the event
design or follow-up. These days many Zoom meetings end with,
"I see there are many more questions in the chat, and many of
you wanted to speak, but there is no more time. Please send us all
the questions you have; we will answer and organize another call."
However, most of the time none of this happens. We are beginning
to play with ways to maintain the learning momentum that call upon
the facilitation practices of Open Space Technology[2] and the best of
what works in the virtual space. For example, instead of ending the
meetings with empty promises, we announce the following: "The next
three weeks this Zoom Room will open every week on this day at the
same time. The link and the password will also be the same. It is a free
and open space for all of you who were here today. Use it for whatever you need it. We will be here offering a simple moderating service
if needed. We do not want you to send us your questions or join any
platform, just show up next week at the same time and day to keep
talking to each other if you want to. We will also play the role of
sending you the weekly highlights of these open space discussions."

**Internet Connection Troubles – There Will Always Be Internet
Connection Troubles:** Connectivity is often an issue. When convening a global learning event this can be due to accessibility and
affordability of the internet, the urban/rural inequities experienced
across the world, or simply nasty weather conditions (i.e., monsoons
or winter blizzards) which are increasing in nastiness due to climate
change. Video requires a lot of bandwidth; if not required, do not
use it. Participants might need to travel to publicly accessible internet connection sites. Consider this when determining the announced
time of learning sessions and whether or not someone is being asked

to travel beyond the safety and security of their home at a particularly insecure time of day.

Let Go of Traditional Ways of Delivery – Get Outside your Comfort Zone: Subject matter experts are essential to robust learning inquiries and might be accustomed to preparing and delivering long presentations followed by Q&A sessions. We observe this dampens the learning inquiry and participatory dialogue. We also recognize that in the relative privacy of one's own home it's easy to read emails or watch birds outside the window. We have found it helpful to work with subject matter experts to chisel down presentations to key messages with explicit practical examples within an 8-10 minute window.

Difficult to Sense Feedback or Ignite Discussion: We are getting more comfortable with our inability to read facial expressions or body language in the virtual space — in fact it can be misleading. There is also the $1/200^{th}$ or some such nanosecond delay built into working virtually. This creates hesitancy. Play with asking people directly for feedback of a learning inquiry question. As facilitators this runs contrary to our participatory practice, as we are often coached not to call on any individual publicly. We have been playfully using prompting language such as, "In a few moments, I am going to call upon three people to weigh in on what they just heard" as a segue to directly calling upon people to participate or provide feedback. We are still working on this one!

It Can Look More Effortless than it Really is: From a logistical point of view, it has become much easier, but developing meaningful and rich 90-120 minute learning sessions requires a considerable amount of preparation. We have found inviting co-design with a representative group of participants enriches the outcomes considerably. This implies pre-engagement, constant finetuning and readjusting learning objectives, landing on the two or three key learning inquiry questions, and even dry runs. The planning needs to be approached with flexibility and humour. Remember participants are not only learning about the technical topic being explored, but are also learning about learning design! Also be aware it is challenging to get a second chance in the Zoom Room. If a critical mass of participants become confused, it can be challenging to regain some semblance of order.

Invitation to Innovate

We are too deeply immersed in the wonder of ongoing learning to offer any definitive conclusions. Our intention in this essay was to share inspirations and ongoing inquiries. Based on our experience, we see incredible possibilities and potential to continue innovating with virtual global networking and dialogue for learning and change. Perhaps our best conclusion is inviting you to reach out and share your success stories with others — tips and tricks, as well as bottle-necks and challenges!

Endnotes

1 Kolb, D.A. and Fry, R.E. (1974). Toward an Applied Theory of Experiential Learning. Cambridge, MA: Alfred P. Sloan School of Management.

2 Open Space Technology: http://openspaceworld.org/wp2/what-is/

High Resolution full colour images of the illustrations in this essay are available on the book's webpage at
http://www.pdltd.net/sprouting-seeds-of-radical-education

Point your smartphone camera at the QR code below to link you directly to the images.

— Nineteen —

Talking the walk: Facilitating learning to build peoples' institutions

CS Reddy, India; Anuj Jain and David Fletcher, Canada

The three of us have each been development practitioners for more than 30 years! Much of our work has involved walking the road of promoting sustainable people's institutions — with all the bumps, potholes and washed-out sections along the way. We have been walking in the field in India, Ethiopia, Thailand, Ghana and many other places. Recently we stepped back to reflect on our learning, specifically about facilitating learning to help build people's institutions.

During our Zoom calls we decided to focus on APMAS[1] in Hyderabad, India, which has championed self-help groups and strengthened people's organizations in India for two decades. We all have a connection to APMAS — CS Reddy, as founder and Chief Executive Officer; Anuj Jain, as long time supporter and thinking partner; and David Fletcher, as a learning consultant. What follows is a reconstruction of our conversation about how seeds of radical education have sprouted in the purpose of building people's organizations.

The Foundation of APMAS

David: APMAS is in the midst of celebrating its 20th anniversary in 2021. Congratulations! What has been important during this time in how you trained people to build people's organizations?

CS: My involvement in participatory training originated from CARE International in India, particularly with Dr. Stephen J. Atwood, so I am thankful to them for seeding many ideas. As a development professional the idea of participatory development, participatory learning and participatory rural appraisal systems was introduced in the early 1990s when I was with CARE in Delhi, and later in Hyderabad.

When I founded APMAS, I insisted all trainings must be partici-patory and built on adult learning principles. I deeply believed in the empowerment of marginalized communities. If we believe in people taking responsibility and being accountable, then a participatory methodology is the way to go. We built on the work of Participatory Research in Asia (PRIA) and Mysore Resettlement and Development Agency (MYRADA), both well-known NGOs in India. We had a Telugu translation of the PRIA training manual on participatory training methodologies. We produced 1,000 copies of that book and distributed it to everyone who attended our training of trainers (TOT) program. Participatory methodologies are not about know-ledge transfer, but about empowerment, active learning and shared responsibility. They became part of our DNA because APMAS was predominantly a capacity building and an enabling and mentoring organization. We push participatory methodologies. When you want women — who are part of the self-help groups (SHGs), federations, co-operative financial institutions or farmer producer organizations — to be strong, you must practice participatory methodology. If not, then women's ability to take leadership, their ability to engage in processes that promote self-help, self-responsibility, democracy, autonomy and independence will be stifled.

David: What were some of the positive impacts of those approaches?

CS: In the initial years of APMAS we did not do any field imple-mentation. Our role was predominantly capacity building of promoters of SHGs and their federations. We created a large pool of around 250 district level resource persons (DRPs), all trained as trainers on participatory methodologies and SHGs. We ran residen-tial training programs for them across Andhra Pradesh state. Many people say they use group discussions, role play, case studies, simu-lations, and so on, but it was important for our participants to understand the adult learning cycle and adult learning principles that were our starting point.

Some DRPs say because of that training, they still have a job today at a senior level. It set a strong foundation and made them commit-ted to the theory of change and transformation that is needed to work with communities to help them build their own strong institutions.

Our residential trainings had songs, dance, collage and celebration. During the residential TOTs, participants enjoyed their learning process and were 100% involved in preparing for their practice sessions at night. These were always eight or ten-day programs. What was unique was — not only did DRPs go through the adult learning principles, the action reflection and learning cycle, methods, and how to use them — they did practice sessions that were videotaped. They would then watch their videos and receive feedback. Sometimes the video feedback session would go up to as late as 11 o'clock at night, such was the enthusiasm!

These 250 people, plus another 20 people from APMAS, were like an army who trained around 10,000 people. These trainers created their own charts, songs, games, exercises, and further improvised learning methods that promoted participation.

David: What impact did this approach have within APMAS itself?

CS: We created a culture of learning, sharing and working together. The entire process of facilitation and training with government staff was always more rigorous. We had the best trainers. During the first five years, if anyone left the organization they always found the best jobs, because they were able to impress upon others what it takes to build a sustainable, self-reliant people's institution based on the values of self-help, mutuality and self-reliance. This participatory methodology and philosophy are interrelated with people's institutions that are democratic, autonomous self-reliant business organizations.

Designing and Delivering Courses – Mutual Learning between the Coady and APMAS

David: Let's fast forward a few years. Anuj, you worked with CARE in India, Zambia, USA, Thailand and elsewhere and were involved in many big, innovative programs. When you joined the Coady International Institute to teach in 2010 you invited CS to join you. Why?

Anuj: When I arrived, I realized all the work that had been done in creating people's institutions by the Coady and in the Antigonish Movement. It pulled me back to focus on building people's institutions for financial and economic inclusion. I agreed to offer a certificate course called *Community Based Microfinance for Financial Inclusion*. It was natural to ask CS to co-facilitate because he lives those principles, and always implements them. CS is a farmer at heart, a people's person; he not only talks about it, he actually puts force behind it and gets things done. I knew he would bring credibility to the Coady's work in current times. He accepted graciously and fell in love with the Coady. So, I want to ask him, "What stands out for you now after almost 10 years of coming to the Coady?"

CS: First was the drive to Antigonish from Halifax. I was excited to come to a small university town. The drive was mesmerizing because I am a nature lover. Then when I came to the new Coady building, the environment was very soothing. People were warm, loving, welcoming. Anyone you said hi to in the corridors extended a warm welcome, gave a big smile and chatted. The air was so fresh and there was little traffic! Coming from Hyderabad, a polluted city with chaotic traffic, to Antigonish was a wonderful place to relax, refresh, rethink and re-energize.

David: And the classroom experiences?

CS: I love the systematic approach of an academic institution. In the Coady, it was very methodical. I liked the energy. In the first two years, it took some time for us to fine tune and co-facilitate. We were constantly asking ourselves and the participants, "What does this mean to you? How does it relate to your work back home?" I was in the mode of experience sharing, so I thought we nicely complemented each other. Anuj brought the global perspective and I was able to bring in case study experiences from India — real examples from the field — with tools and methodologies that worked. That was a wonderful experience. I was always learning from the exercises we did, the conversations, even in the corridors. With case study reading materials, we used to have debates and discussions.

Anuj and I did a lot of innovation in an evolving methodology, going beyond the manual but starting with some structure, a small class size, a classroom setting that was flexible, and that automatically promoted participation. For example, in India participants tend to call everyone "sir." At the Coady we called each other by first names, so there was egalitarianism in the class. Anuj always brought candy into the room or flowers to decorate, which created a wonderful learning environment and broke hierarchical barriers. We had structured sessions, but we almost always deviated from the plan and broke rules. We never believed that rules were always the best things to follow, but having them to start was important.

Anuj: CS also brought something special to the classroom: a manner that is authentic, natural, not put on. That is his biggest value. His sharing was so connected with people's own experiences and lives that it immediately brought credibility to the conversations.

From a methods point of view, we introduced several things. One example is the debate methodology leading to synthesizing learning around contentious issues which showed there is no one right answer. We posed, "Should SHGs federate or not?" or "Does microfinance really create women's empowerment?" We used that method and pushed people against each other, and then through synthesizing as a group, we would come to realize that reality was somewhere in the middle.

We introduced field visits to a farm. This started when we were out for our morning walk and CS waved to this farming family, busy doing early morning chores. We became friends and soon after they invited our participants to visit their farm, which is a member of the local Scotsburn dairy co-operative. It was such a critical exposure for the group from many developing economies. They learned what a small farming family looks like and how farmers continue to struggle even in Canada to maintain their small farm status.

In the classroom, we truly behaved like "learner facilitators." There was great equality, but not one point of view. We never felt shy about challenging each other in front of the class. If we had a different point of view, we presented it respectfully; this made it authentic for people. We both genuinely believe in building people's institutions, so I think that became our fulcrum. No matter what the method was I think people saw our commitment to building people's organizations.

CS: Using participatory methods for building institutions became the culture, the religion of what we did at APMAS. It sounded very much like courses at the Coady. Participatory methods created a culture of respect, listening and challenging each other. Sharing authentically with other practitioners was its richness; it was not a tool or technique, it was the overall cultural approach that made a difference. Since starting APMAS, I realized I had to believe in people and their knowledge.

Anuj: So, we are not just teachers?

CS: We are, and we should be willing to learn. We should be willing to understand participants' constraints, their challenges, their circumstances, particularly when we talk about women's empowerment and savings and credit groups: owned, managed, controlled and used by women. The belief that women can lead organizations was fundamental to our work. If you are talking about community based microfinance, self-help is fundamental. When you want to promote self-help, mutuality and respect in co-operatives, then one person, one vote is fundamental, as is the belief in democracy.

Anuj: We could not do anything less in the classroom. The processes that are critical for building people's institutions include believing in their innate capability, experiences and their decision-making ability. Appreciating the community is important, while challenging members to embrace a system that will enable them to be perpetual organizations. They are not just there for a month or a year, but forever. In our classroom and field experience, we always had this resonance of the philosophy and values of participatory methodology and co-operative institutions. These principles were mutually reinforcing.

David: How was that received? In the classroom we have people with different levels of education, different experiences and from different countries and contexts. What was your sense of how the principles and values you were promoting were received?

CS: People came with a lot of hunger for learning, open minds and a lot of questions and experiences. They came not only with a willingness to learn, but a willingness to share. Anuj ensured there was adequate opportunity for participants to share their best practices, their experiences, their learning and their innovations.

In terms of the participatory methodology, I think the participants loved it. We had these distinct organizational models. In India, they are called self-help groups, in Africa village savings and loan associations. In both, the idea is that the models must ensure transparency, accountability and services to members, not profitability. In many courses, we had staff from microfinance institutions as participants. By the end they became transformed. They said, "We didn't know that community-based microfinance is actually empowering, enabling, building and going beyond the so-called delivery of microfinance." There are different perspectives: government officers coming from a service delivery perspective; NGOs coming from a women's empowerment perspective; and bankers coming from a financial inclusion perspective. All these perspectives are valid.

Anuj: When I first joined the Coady, I was not fully aligned with the diversity of people in the classroom. A lot of work went into this. We must have spent hours re-designing the course and going back to this fundamental idea of community-based institutions for people's own economic freedom. Not many people in the general public understand that SHGs are innovations over co-operatives. Co-operatives became too management and governance oriented, where power fell into the hands of a few people. SHGs are brilliant innovations — keeping it small so that everybody has the chance, the flexibility and the convenience to participate. Those SHGs can also be brought together to take advantage of an economy of scale that the co-operatives have.

People often came to the course to find answers, but we told them, "You must find your own answers." What you will get is an exposure to what is happening in the world. A big part of the course was the learning project. They had to come up with a learning question on day three of the course and then pursue the answers to that question. We also created a small game where we distributed an equal number of small wooden coins to every participant. Every time someone learned from another participant, they would immediately give coins to that person. It was amazing validation for the person who got those coins.

David: What else were you seeing at the Coady that was valuable to APMAS and your work?

CS: We watched what others were doing. We saw sessions using the Margolis Wheel,[2] for example, and used it in our final session for peer feedback. We also picked up the World Café method.[3] We were always hungry to improvise our methodology and the learning environment for the participants.

We were curious about the excitement always coming from the *Certificate in Community Development Leadership by Women* facilitated by Debbie Castle and Emily Sikazwe. The women were always animated. I would be jealous because they had these colorful charts on the wall and were always creating things. So, Anuj and I would have a big discussion and say, "We are too content oriented, we need room for creative expression. Learning must be liberating, empowering and enabling."

Continuing to Learn Together – Participatory Capacity Building with APMAS

Anuj: David, when you were directing education programs at the Coady and first met CS what were your first impressions, and how did that lead to your work with APMAS over the last few years in India?

David: I remember the great enthusiasm CS showed, his willingness to ask questions about programs overall, and really engage with what was going on. He was curious about what we were doing in the facilitation course and was interested in getting a copy of our manual. I heard about the interactions with the women's certicate and the initiative you both had to say, "Okay, let's find out what the excitement is about." Debbie and I had been going to India on an annual basis and CS invited us to Hyderabad to co-facilitate a two-day session, and things developed from there. It has been an organic evolving relationship.

CS: The reason I wanted you both involved was that I knew when a new person comes reflection becomes more effective. I knew I would not have to manage you as foreign consultants and I could convert myself into a participant. Your facilitation of those sessions with participants from the National Institute of Rural Development, the Management Development Institute, and other NGOs was refreshing, and I thought it made people become better at what they are doing by learning from each other.

David: I remember feeling a bit nervous about working with all these highly experienced practitioners and thinking we needed to offer more theory about the processes and methodologies. In conversations with you, you were always determined just to bring them together to reflect on their practice. You reminded us to focus on the process of interacting with them. In the first warmup activity, everybody was standing and sharing with each other and chatting enthusiastically. It was clear the people who were there had enthusiasm, commitment and hunger to improve their practice and it would be an amazing group to work with.

Anuj: How are those participants practicing what they learned through reflection with Debbie and David?

CS: They now do more thinking when designing their sessions. There was a lasting impression about preparing well for a session, and not getting too carried away by how much we need to cover. A lot of the methods people were exposed to have become part of our self-learning modules for the Farmer Producer Organizations (FPOs). New modules are being developed everywhere. David and Debbie made our APMAS team think about a participant-centred approach to learning. Now we use the word learning, rather than training, "How do we make this session a learning experience?" They also like to do more outdoors. The static style of sitting around a table with a lot of PowerPoint slides is changing; now there is more movement, getting off the chairs, integrating trust building and other kinds of exercises. We did these exercises before, but now they are more diverse and most importantly, they have a deeper understanding about participation and unlearning. The practitioners are more confident in conducting sessions and less anxious about facilitation.

David: In all three sessions we have done with APMAS, there has always been lots of practice. We use video for feedback, which you said you did early in your work, and we do a "hot seat" for peer feedback where people try to really hone and polish their skills to take them to another level.

Have you found that idea of constantly improving themselves, trying new things, taking risks and then getting feedback makes a difference?

CS: Absolutely. They use video a lot more, recording two-minute synthesis statements from group members. We are also producing more videos so farmers' organizations will have a series of them for learning approaches and regulations.

Anuj: David, can you say more about your learning experience with these highly experienced participants. What was your impression about their level of engagement, commitment and curiosity?

David: It was different for the different groups we worked with. In the first two-day session with APMAS and the NGO group, it was obvious they had worked with these kinds of tools before. They had already done a lot with women, farmers and people in communities to make their sessions engaging, but there was a hunger to learn and do new things. I remember one participant who had been doing these kinds of activities for more than 30 years had some deep questions: "Is it really making a difference? Is this really the kind of stuff we need to do after 30 years?" Other participants had just started a new management institute and were curious about what they could do to make the place unique; they were taking lots of notes, sharing their manuals and wanting comments. That first interaction was exciting in terms of the willingness people had to reflect on their own practice. I think we called the course Invigorating Your Teaching Methods, and they were very keen on doing that.

On our second visit we did a three-day session with a group of academics. They were engaged, but it was clear they came from a different perspective. It was not about being a practitioner in the field, but rather about being a content expert in the classroom. They were terribly busy with all the programs going on, so it was a different kind of interest and motivation. The contrast between the NGO group working in the field and this group showed how constraining institutional settings can be. They were interested to learn and do things differently, there was great leadership there, and a desire for efforts to be values-based, but an institution can really put constraints on the space people have in their heads for learning. For us, it was a great sense of recognition that in India there are huge contrasts between the levels where people work and the different kinds of interactions and interventions that can make a difference.

CS: Now you have done a third session. It is always good to have continuous engagement because learning and facilitation is a continuous process. David and Debbie have a wonderful way of influencing people to look at alternative ways to make facilitation more effective, more impactful. That is why I feel in the years to come, the engagement needs to be ongoing. Then facilitation and learning can become more effective and that will strengthen the institutions of the farmers.

Is This Work Radical?

Anuj: How is this radical, or specifically helpful to creating people's institutions? Is it still relevant in the 21st century?

CS: Having seen the Antigonish Movement and co-operatives created by Coady graduates in other countries, it gives me confidence the approach we are pursuing in India is the correct one. It is different than what many others are doing. The emphasis must be on democracy, autonomy, independence and self-reliance. It is also clear that building membership-based people's organizations around economic activity, but not exclusively economic activity, takes time. It does not happen overnight — patient, committed, process-oriented facilitation is needed to build long-term sustainable institutions. In India, we tend to be in a hurry, or expect it should happen in a three-year project cycle, but building self-reliant people's organizations takes time. That is abundantly clear to me now. Going slow can be radical. I find absolutely no reason why one should compromise on values and principles. How do we live the co-operative values and principles? How do we practice them on a day-to-day basis? In adult education, a participant-centric approach is important. We cannot impose rules, regulations and structures. We need to be evolving and open-minded.

My self-confidence has gone up over the past 10 years because I can see it more clearly. As a practitioner and facilitator, even when I conduct a staff meeting, I am now more participatory. When I make a field visit, I now listen better. This idea of listening to and learning from people and being willing to change is powerful. Many people will say this, but we have to constantly challenge ourselves to practice it. This journey has helped me broaden my perspective and deepen the approach we have in APMAS. Many organizations in India seem to appreciate APMAS sessions on values and principles. Our strong push for SHG federations to be self-regulating, for example, is all about how to practice the values and principles of democratically run people's institutions. We, at APMAS, are constantly learning, improving, and influencing how to make these federations important community-owned economic and social institutions, self-managed and self-governed. This is not the norm. With our steadfast belief in participatory methodologies, we have also influenced many World Bank and Department for International Development funded projects which are implemented by governments. Now the projects all practice participatory training methodology and are process-oriented in promoting sustainable people's institutions.

David: You mentioned participant-centered process facilitation. I think that is very much how I tend to identify myself and I think Debbie would as well. It is a concept that has been around for a long time, and in its own way is very radical. In addition, there is this sense of trusting the ability and the desire of people to want to learn, and through that learning to understand better, then to make decisions and choices to improve their situation in a just way. That focus on learning is very central to what we have been involved in.

As you said, CS, a values-driven, principled approach to setting up organizations is so important for organizational effectiveness, organizational development and organizational learning. It starts with individuals and those individuals in dialogue with each other. That is where the real learning takes place, and that learning transforms individuals and shifts relationships between individuals. Then people in those relationships can set up institutions and sustain them. There needs to be structures, systems and accountability, but it is the values and principles that must be set in the foundation. You can not have people's institutions and FPOs until that foundation is set. I have learned a lot about that from you and APMAS.

CS: I am also deeply thankful to Debbie because every time she is at APMAS, the women staff get excited. She is a source of inspiration. It brings back into focus APMAS being a women's organizations. How do we be more women-centric, even though our work was with all women organizations. Now as we move to farmers' organizations, there tends to be more men. Debbie reminds us to maintain our women-centric principles. So that reminder has been unbelievably valuable. Both Debbie and David's involvement strengthens my hand because staff feel inspired and creative. Their batteries are generally recharged for six months!

I think now the task for all of us in these pandemic times is how to continue our passion to promote participatory methodologies through capacity building, developing learning modules and policy advocacy. The ENABLE network is a national network for enabling the SHG movement and APMAS has taken on the responsibility of promoting self-regulation among the SHG federations and FPOs.[4]

How do we continue to promote values-based learning systems using new tools? The power of technology can be harnessed. Yet we must be participatory, even though we are not physically there. It is a big challenge!

Anuj: It is something we can work on together! To continue to walk the talk of using participatory engagement processes to build authentic peoples' institutions.

Endnotes

1 APMAS is the name of a not-for-profit society established to promote self-reliant people's institutions. Originally named the Mahila Abhivruddhi Society Andra Pradesh it has now expanded to other parts of India and developing countries and is simply known as APMAS.

2 Description of Margolis Wheel available at www.pdltd.net/list-of-facilitation-tools

3 Description of World Café available at www.pdltd.net/list-of-facilitation-tools

4 ENABLE: www.apmas.org/enable.php

[The desire for knowledge] has gripped the people en masse, and without regard to condition, class or circumstances...

Now that peace has come, they seek an equal share in opportunity and in the good and worthwhile things of life. Disabilities and unjust inequalities, scarcely realized in times past by the very victims, or if realized borne with dull resignation, have now come to the attention of all and they must be redressed.

Rev. James (Father Jimmy) Tompkins
Knowledge for the People, 1921

The graphics created for this book considered the authors spread around the world; our rootedness in transformative learning and change; the role of diverse environments in shaping our lives; and, the feeling of marginalization some authors have experienced based on their commitment to change. The dandelion is common in many countries and a socially "marginalized" sprout in some, but actually a sprout that matures with every part having a beautiful and delicious use. The four images capture the essence of each section of the book, and represent the binding beauty of the whole.

Darren C Brown

Twenty

Closing thoughts: Honour the sprouting seeds around you

Once seeds have sprouted, they require sufficient amounts of water and sunlight to grow into mature plants bearing leaves, blossoms and fruits. This is also true of initiatives based in the principles of radical education. The stories you have read in this collection represent how people around the world are nurturing transformative change, growing health and vibrancy for themselves and their communities — the fruits of their labours. This sample of experiences reflects a microcosm of the diversity and passion that goes into every effort to help shift the world towards a more peaceful, just and equitable place.

Gratitude to all the authors who have contributed their stories! Bringing this collection of insights together has been truly inspirational. We have all learned through the experiences of these dedicated practitioner-authors in the fields of adult education, community and organizational development, social action and human transformation. With so many different contexts, it's wonderful to remember our classroom experiences together where all of these contexts would be used in generative ways to push our thinking and practices to new considerations and new ways of improving the lives of community people. Imagine all of the authors in the same workshop, provided with a platform that starts with them and their own experiences, encourages critical reflection and listening to others, and works towards collective action and planning. Their rich stories emulate the educational processes that can ultimately change the world.

The essays provide examples of the seeds of radical education that have sprouted and are making a difference. There are distinct and powerful themes recurring throughout the essays that demonstrate how radical education can be translated into sustainable change in today's world. Here are some of those themes.

Many authors offered insights from their personal journeys of transformation, sharing reflections on how they faced and overcame the challenges they met, and what they learned from those experiences.

Several identified the role of mothers, mentors and Elders in inspiring their commitment to helping others at an early age, particularly those who are economically, socially and politically marginalized in their societies. Authors wrote of mothers and grandmothers who helped break stereotypes, protected watersheds and the environment and became leaders for future generations. Authors learned about their culture, history and values, and observed how their mentors displayed resilience, perseverance and co-operation in the face of poverty and historic oppression. As readers we were also challenged to think about the danger of blind allegiances to mentors or Elders and to ensure we are always accountable to the people we are expected to serve.

The authors recognized their actions as development practitioners were guided by a shared commitment to achieving social justice and a peaceful world for all to live "a full and abundant life"[1] — a demanding path to navigate in many of their working and living contexts where existing structures, as well as cultural and organizational norms, limit their ability to motivate change.

Many wrote about the transformative effect the Coady experience had on their lives and on their daily practice, particularly learning to embrace and appreciate the humanity in others, and in themselves. Each acknowledged the importance of building authentic relationships of trust, whether within their organizations, families or communities, by keeping their hearts and minds open to learning and listening actively to reach mutual understanding of the way forward.

For some, this journey of ongoing personal transformation also meant questioning one's own education, negotiating new norms and finding common ground with those with very different world views. It also meant working on trauma and developing a new mental model of intergenerational responsibility. The authors shared how learning continues from mistakes and small actions, and includes struggles, grief and resilience. Personal transformation is a constant state of becoming, and opening up free space in hearts, minds and souls so that wounded souls can be regenerated and the joy of living can be reclaimed.

Returning to familiar contexts with new levels of awareness and skills required each one of the practitioner-authors to have deep faith in their own capacity and ability to break the mould of old ways of doing things that no longer created well-being for all. Each story told us of creative ways and means used by the practitioners that offered something significantly different and appropriate for themselves, their colleagues, communities and organizations. Often the very fundamental skills of bringing a group together to collectively determine "what are we seeing and experiencing now in our communities?" and "what would we like to see or experience?" required the creativity and flexibility of these authors who believe in the agency and goodness of people. As we heard in many of the stories the obstacles were many, and the solutions took the practitioner-authors to new places as individuals (physically, mentally and emotionally) and as collectives.

As with Coady, Tompkins, the Sisters of St. Martha[2] and the many generations of co-operative and credit union members in this part of Canada, people move out of oppressive systems in which they find themselves into new territories of collective capacity to value each individual for their own unique talents and worth, not as economic units for production and consumption only.

The essays demonstrate the courage and inspiration of these practitioner-authors to give back to the marginalized and poor communities where they were raised. Their work demonstrates a great caring for their community and the well-being that community members can bring to themselves and their environment using an adult education approach.

The path of a change agent comes with many risks for those who raise their voices when they see injustice and who organize and mobilize others to join them in seeking a better life. It requires fearlessness from the leadership and others who are willing to work together toward a shared vision of a just world. These efforts often meet with resistance from community members who can't afford to take risks, and pushback from those who enjoy the status quo from their privileged position of power and authority in society. It therefore takes persistence, perseverance and sometimes the caution to step back until the time is right to encourage change and overcome suspicion of ulterior motives. Some authors discuss the need to be outspoken in their commitment to the emancipation of marginalized groups, and to step forward into political and social activism. This can result in risk to life, or forced exile, but it is often what it takes to achieve social justice.

In Indigenous and settler communities in Canada, as well as in Egypt, Ghana, Grenada, India, Nepal, Kenya and Zimbabwe, we can visualize the return of these graduates wearing new lenses to look at their old surroundings with a different set of analytical tools. They were able to talk about and use these tools to raise awareness with others of the oppressive structures around them and apply, not just try, but really apply a radical education approach. Much like the work of Joanna Macy[3] and David Korten[4], they were applying holding actions (so things wouldn't get worse); creating alternatives (through dialogue and action), and shifting consciousness (through valuing peace over debate, love over fear and well-being over poverty).

We see in the essays that to heal conflict and build peace a foundation of transformative change in individuals, communities, society and the relationship between human beings and the earth itself is required. Conflict has many faces. Authors wrote how conflict appears in our lives as workplace bullying, conflict over food, water and land, and in the destructive collision of world views. It can be within the self, between individuals, or between communities and nations. There is a shared human history of trauma that requires healing; being listened to is the first step, then people can discover the power they have within to heal themselves and overcome violence, pain and fear. People can then engage in community healing and a revolution of the heart, nurturing cultural revitalization and new mental models of intergenerational responsibility. Healing through art and these new mental models are helping unlearn stereotypes and are making a difference where the practitioner-authors are located. Speaking, breaking cultures of silence, reflecting, analyzing and listening were named many times in the stories as essential ingredients for change to disrupt the norm that marginalizes and leaves so many people out.

To do this the authors lead by example, sharing their space and leadership platform with others of different genders, races, skills, educational and cultural backgrounds. As they revealed their humanness, differences dissolved, and were no longer obstacles but building blocks of a more genuinely inclusive society. In organizations we have seen learning become the magical ingredient that changes hierarchies into conversational circles and intergenerational spaces, that produce meaningful initiatives with the people the organization was created to serve, whether as part of government, business, civil society, or faith-based organizations. The authors and their peers around the world are making a difference one meaningful shift in attitude, knowledge or skill at a time!

Authors recommend participant-centred learning, patient process facilitation and engaging creativity based on a fundamental belief in the innate capabilities that people can find their own answers. As facilitators, they argue to custom design with heart, mind and soul and, when necessary, to put "real life injustice in front of people"[5] for them to work with. They also recommend redesigning when neeeded and when the opportunity arises, and to find safe ways to connect with participants of different spiritualities and different world views. Many suggested living the principles one teaches to give credibil-ity, and to establish a culture of learning and sharing so that stories of critical pedagogy can be woven throughout organizations and in every conversation in people's lives. Respecting diversity is key, while at the same time being careful of what can trigger trauma for people, and recognizing the power of words to empower or disempower. Curiosity needs to be nurtured and collective creativity unleashed so that a revo-lution of the heart can take place that is visually stimulating and fun.

Authors also challenge us to be in a "perpetual state of critical consciousness,"[6] to unlearn the idolizing of institutions and to work to disrupt, dismantle and rebuild. This may include reclaiming and revi-talizing world views that have been disrupted in the past. Unlearning is important so we do not get imprisoned by a single lens/identity and can make a shift to respect diverse views. It demands learning humility and appreciative analysis, going beyond our own beliefs, views, opin-ions or religion, and being open and accepting of different spiritualities. This includes a recognition of the interdependence of all life forms.

One of the most significant and radical themes that came up in the essays was breaking boundaries of all kinds — personal, social, political and cultural. They wrote about overcoming patriarchal and religious stereotypes, about violence, fear and pain after revo-lution, and simply talking about things people never talked about before. Authors discussed the danger of conventional ways of doing things and idolizing institutions, instead giving priority to lived expe-rience and being accountable to people with disabilities and other marginalized groups. They stressed the importance of different spiritualities and respecting indigenous knowledges and ways of revitalizing communities after catastrophic disruptions.

The way forward for those committed to social and ecological justice will continue to be challenging in the coming years. Structural and systemic change takes time and requires leadership in all sectors — government, civil society, business and partnership initiatives at all levels — that is committed to working towards a just world, not toward re-election, profits or short-term fixes. We know that leadership will come from the next generation of change agents in countries around the world where the seeds of radical education are already sprouting and spreading virally among youth through innovative online channels of connectivity. Their energy and passion will drive the next phase of Joanna Macy's Great Turning.

As we met over a Zoom call in the early days of the pandemic, most of the authors found it challenging to call themselves "authors," many coming from oral traditions. We have all been fortunate that Paulo Freire[7], who it is said only wanted to be an equal member of community in making change happen, wrote his story about his experiences in Latin America. On this 100th year after his birth, we celebrate him with our own stories about seeking justice, peace, solidarity, learning, dialogue, accountability, discovery, resilience, transformation and radical education.

Our hope is that you look for the sprouting seeds of radical change around you, honour the changes you see and support them as you can, and look inside to see what seeds of change you are planting. What stage are your personal, community or societal change initiatives in? How are you nurturing them so they are sustainable — strongly rooted, appropriate for local conditions, nurtured as they grow, celebrated when they blossom, and put to gentle rest when their time has come? It is these kinds of ongoing efforts for learning and change that will create the kind of world we choose to have in the future.

Peace.
Olga, Debbie and David

Endnotes

1   Coady, M.M. (1939). Masters of their Own Destiny: The story of the Antigonish Movement of adult education through economic cooperation. New York, NY: Harper & Brothers.

2   Moses Coady, Jimmy Tompkins and the Sisters of St. Martha were the major inspiration behind the Antigonish Movement, a people's movement for socio-economic justice in rural Canada in the 1930s and 1940s that has continued to this day. https://coady.stfx.ca/collection/the-antigonish-movement/

3   Macy, J., & Johnstone, C. (2012). Active Hope: How to face the mess we are in without going crazy. Novato, CA: New World Library.

4   Korten, D.C. (2007). The Great Turning: From empire to each community. San Francisco, CA: Berrett-Koehler.

5   Gad, J. M. (2021). Art for social change and transformation. In this publication, p. 108.

6   Okafo, D. (2021). Finding a road that was always here. In this publication, p. 94.

7   Freire, P. (2000). Pedagogy of the Oppressed. (20th anniversary ed.) New York, NY: Continuum.

Essayists and Editors

Balakrishna Venkatesh (Venky), India

After a long career in development focused on disability rights, development and organizational development, I am currently serving as President of the Community-based Rehabilitation (CBR) Global Network. In this capacity, we initiated a global campaign in 2021 to have CBR recognized in a key World Health Assembly policy statement to ensure "the highest attainable standard of health for persons with disabilities." I am an advisor to WHO on INCLUDE, an online training program using CBR Guidelines and based on core values of self-determination, self-advocacy and inclusion for persons with disabilities. I have provided consulting and training services in more than 30 countries, pioneering ways to mainstream disability into existing rural development initiatives since 1987 based on these core values. Two great achievements in my life are: 1) with Action on Disability and Development India (ADD India) which partnered with more than 180 NGOs that are impacting the lives of over 100,000 persons with different disabilities and their families; and, 2) with a cross disability district federation in Andhra Pradesh India which has a total membership of 28,000 persons with different disabilities. Each office of the federation is held by persons with different disabilities and is well-represented by women with or without disabilities.

Darren C Brown, Canada

Born, raised and living on Jeddore Harbour, Nova Scotia at an edge of the beginning of the North Atlantic, the patterns and cycles of Nature shape who I am. Facilitating harmonious, just and sustainable learning and change within richly diverse and complex communities and organizations defines my creative professional passion. The desired result of my work is to secure just inclusion, promote equity and advance participatory learning experiences. I am a trained graphic facilitator and integrate graphic techniques and visual elements into collaborative learning and thinking designs. I have been working nationally, internationally and interculturally for over 30 years.

Deborah (Debbie) Castle (Co-editor), Canada

Being an editor of writers in a collective is a new-found love of mine! I have co-authored several books in the spiritual domain and been co-editor of this Seeds to Sprouts series. I currently think of myself as a soul having a human experience and truly appreciate the level of engagement with all those involved in this creative project. As a founder and community partner with People Development Limited, I participate as a lead consultant on learning inquiries and strategic thinking conversations with people in organizations in the Americas, Asia and Africa. 2021 has been a remarkable year of taking our facilitation skills online and discovering we can create an intimate environment to explore the potential and possibilities inherent in all our relations. I am very appreciative of time spent in realizing my master's and doctoral studies and having a meditation practice as the foundation of my understanding. It's an honour to work with this group of writers.

Shaiju Chacko, India

I am a priest of the Catholic Diocese of Jammu-Srinagar in the Union Territory of Jammu & Kashmir in the north of India. I joined the development sector in 2006. In 2011, I earned a Master's in Social Work from the University of Delhi and participated in the Coady International Institute's *Diploma in Development Leadership* the same year. Upon returning from the Coady, I joined the ambitious employable skill development project of the Central Government as Project Co-ordinator for Don Bosco Tech Society (DB Tech). The aim of the project was to provide employable skills to school and college dropouts. DB Tech, as an implementing partner, has been instrumental in training more than 18,000 youth of Jammu & Kashmir, a region known for extreme anti-government sentiments and active militancy for decades. This project opened new opportunities for youth of diverse backgrounds to come together. As a priest, it was a journey of self-discovery and meaningful engagement with multiple stakeholders ranging from community members to government officials. In 2015, I took charge as Director of the Catholic Social Service Society, the social organ of the Diocese. This responsibility helped me reach out to the rural folk, particularly women of self-help groups to guide them in setting up livelihood options while engaging with different programs of the organization. In 2018, I received an opportunity to return to the Coady as a Fellow to reflect on my journey and how the Coady experience helped me navigate the complexities of the region and shape me as a leader.

David Fletcher (Co-editor), Canada

I have been involved in community development and social justice work since the 1980s. Over the years I have had the privilege to work with people wanting to create a better world in Nigeria, Canada, South Africa, The Gambia, Ethiopia, Ghana, Kenya, China, Nepal, India and a few other places along the way. I work as a facilitator and adult educator and have been applying those skills in sectors such as community health, rural development, anti-racist education, personal change, youth leadership, advocacy, food sovereignty, and the revitalization of indigenous knowledges. Indigenous knowledges is one of my greatest interests, for which I earned a PhD degree in 2018 from the University for Development Studies, Ghana, for research with the Dagara people. I have played many roles over the years with civil society organizations and universities: from consultant to project officer, program manager to education director. From 2007 to 2019 I was full-time senior teaching staff with the Coady International Institute and served as Director of Education. Since leaving the Institute, I have become a partner in People Development Ltd. In this capacity I have worked with the African Nova Scotian community, various NGOs in India, and continue to support social justice movements on the African continent and elsewhere. I continue to write and have a strong meditation practice which I am happy to share with others. I am keen to help people use video technologies in documenting and reporting on their work for change.

John Milad Gad, Egypt

I am an Egyptian artist, combining many roles in my work — I am a director, an actor, an educator, an author, an art therapist, a narrator, a screenwriter and an advocate. Bringing learning, the arts and healing together led to the development of Art for Social Change and Transformation, the approach I developed after years of working to help people express their deepest hurts and sufferings. I write about this approach in my essay in this book. I founded an artistic

troupe called 'WeLessa' (There is Still More), whose performances
address issues of human rights and freedoms, especially those of
immigrants, women and rural people in Egypt. In our work we help
people understand and overcome the challenges they face in daily
life. With new understanding, people develop re-enactments of the
violence they have experienced and rise to new levels of self-awareness
and community strength. In 2014, it was a great honour in my life
to be awarded a prize for supporting civil society using the arts from
the Clinton Global Initiative and to have President Obama publicly
appreciate my work during a gathering hosted by the United Nations.

Ehab Gamal, Egypt

I am a political and social activist and Human Rights Defender
(HRD) from Egypt. Committed to social development and inclusive change, I hold a Bachelor of Law from Cairo University, and a
Diploma in Civil Society and Human Rights from the Faculty of
Economics and Political Science also from Cairo University. I have
studied and been mentored in governance, transparency and accountability, community facilitation and youth leadership. For this, I have
been awarded certificates from the Coady International Institute
of St. Francis Xavier University in *Transparency, Accountability and
Governance* and *Global Youth Leadership.* I am a past recipient of the
Lazord Fellowship for Civic Leadership at the American University in
Cairo. I have been working in civil society since 2008 and helped to
co-found and manage various youth NGOs, as well as diverse spaces
and movements in Egypt and the Middle East before being forced
into optional political exile since 2017. I am currently in charge
of the Youth Driving Change program at one of Denmark's largest privately funded child rights organizations and am studying for a
master's degree in Global Studies and International Development at
Roskilde University in Copenhagen.

Nawal Ghatas, Egypt

I am the founder and chairperson of Haddouta Mesreya Association.
My interest and work is mainly focused on transformative learning
and adult education, inspired by my learning journey at the Coady in
2007. It completely captured my whole attention and motivated me
to pursue my MA. I value and appreciate working with disadvantaged

people regardless of their background, education, social status, or religion. I enjoy facilitating the process of helping people to perceive themselves, others and the world around them to create a meaningful life. I am privileged to be working and volunteering with adult learners for more than 20 years with different organizations inside and outside Egypt, including as a facilitator for four years with a Coady project in Egypt on transparency, accountability in good governance. The facilitation journey continues with Coady graduates especially in Haddouta Mesreya and other NGOs. Previously, for six years, I was a program manager with Coptic Orphans where I implemented several initiatives including professional training and awareness programs. Before that, I enjoyed working with adults as a teacher in the Theological College for two years. Gifted with an adventurous spirit, adoring traveling, exploring and learning about and from different cultures, I volunteered in five countries in Sub-Saharan Africa, Nepal, India, and USA with women, youth and refugees. Being a lifelong learner, I hold an MA in Higher, Adult and Lifelong Education from Michigan State University, a *Diploma in Development Leadership* from the Coady, a BA in Theology, and a BS in Agriculture. My learning journey continues for a deeper understanding of myself and the world around me.

Olga Gladkikh (Co-editor), Canada

I'm an Advocacy and Citizen Engagement specialist with more than 35 years of diversified experience as an adult educator and communications practitioner. This includes overseas consultancies with local, national and international NGOs in Asia, Africa, South Pacific, Caribbean, Eastern Europe, as well the US and Canada. After a long association with the Coady Institute, I am currently a co-creator with People Development Ltd., a Canadian consultancy group that specializes in people-centered development (www.pdltd.net). The main focus of my work is to help citizens and their organizations strengthen their capacity, agency and voice to influence change and to participate actively in the decisions that affect their lives and livelihoods. I have an MA in Journalism and a BA (Honours) in Psychology, both from the University of Western Ontario, and completed course work and research towards a PhD in Adult Education from the University of Nottingham in the UK. I stand in solidarity with change agents around the world who contribute toward achieving a just world for all within their own spheres of influence and action.

Anuj Jain, Canada

Joining the Coady International Institute in 2010 was a turning point for me. I was moving away from direct implementation and becoming an educator, reflecting with other community-based practitioners and exploring the meanings of leadership for social change. The Coady became the place to meet many exceptional development leaders and educators, many who have become lifelong friends. I am glad to be part of this book of reflections of our individual and collective journeys, spreading the seeds of transformative education. I now manage Facilitators for Social Change, incubating disruptive/innovative ideas and managing learning partnerships, globally and at home in Antigonish. My development sector journey started by accident, when I joined Participatory Research in Asia (PRIA) in India in 1987 after doing an MBA and not wanting to sell soap or fax machines. My perspectives about life, communities, gender, inequity, poverty, and social justice changed completely. At PRIA I learned about adult transformative learning as the basis of social change and had the chance to be part of the women's Self-Help Group Movement in its formative years. I joined CARE in 1991 and engaged in several small and large scale programs for women's economic empowerment. The experience from India paved the way to go to Zambia, and then USA, to work with CARE's global portfolio in the economic sector, furthering programming for rural and local market systems across Africa, Asia, Middle-East and Latin America. I also managed a portfolio of CARE's programs in Asia from 2005-10 in the health, education, food security, disaster management, financial and economic inclusion sectors, based out of Thailand. I continue to engage in several community initiatives, and live with my wife Jyotsna in Antigonish.

Pamela Johnson, Canada

I am currently employed as a faculty member of Conestoga College in the Community and Social Services Management Graduate Program. I have a strong desire to see greater equity and access for all. My interests have led me to work and research into securing sustainable and good housing for people living with disabilities, and in building a strong intersectional analysis and broader representation of content and materials in the classroom. I was attracted to working at the Coady International Institute initially because of my family's roots in the co-operative and credit union movements in the Acadian region of Prince Edward Island. While at the Coady, I worked as a Program Teaching Staff in the International Centre for Women's Leadership. My fondest memories are of my time in the classroom and of my collaborations with graduates of the program, which both left an indelible mark on my heart and strongly influenced my continued work in social justice. I hold an MBA in Community Economic Development, a degree in Psychology, and have completed course work for a master's degree in Social Work and Counselling. I am experienced in developing participatory action research in both local and international contexts, and have been invited to speak as a panelist focusing on my work on gender, disability, the application of intersectional analysis and participatory action research.

Bashiratu Kamal, Ghana
I hold a master's degree in Labor and Global Workers Rights with a minor in Adult Education from Pennsylvania State University, a degree in Human Resource Management, a Coady *Diploma in Development Leadership* and an Advanced Diploma in Journalism. I hold several other certificates in Inclusiveness, Diversity and No Discrimination in the World of Work; Youth Leadership; Gender and Development; Gender Equality and Mutual Gains Negotiations; and, Gender and Organizational Development. I am a cohort of the Ghanaian Women's Social Leadership Program at the Robert F. Wagner Institute of New York University. I am a feminist and unionist who works as a Gender and Labour Expert with the General Agricultural Workers' Union (GAWU) of the Trades Union Congress-Ghana (TUC). I spearheaded constitutional amendments to create women's structures that ensure their visibility and integration in the Union and developed the Union's first gender policy in 2016. I lead various Union campaigns on the provision of child care facilities at the workplace, strengthening maternity protection, occupational safety and health and eliminating violence and sexual harassment in the workplace. I have held leadership positions as a student, serving

as the Women's Commissioner of the National Union of Ghana
Students in 2008 and the Assistant Secretary of the National Youth
Council of the TUC. I was instrumental in the establishment of the
National Youth Council and the development of the gender and
youth policies of the TUC in 2012 and 2016.

Cynthia Khoury, Egypt

I am an independent trainer, facilitator and graphic facilitator. I
worked at CIDA in Egypt for 15 years in project management and
monitoring the implementation of working plans. I have also been
a Scout leader for more than 25 years. I am passionate about working with people at all levels, seeing development happening in them
and being part of this change, so people can be "masters of their own
destiny." I have always been doing some kind of facilitation with children and youth through different educational programs through
volunteer work nationally and internationally. My experience at
the Coady International Institute as a participant and a co-facilitator was a turning point for me as it grounded my facilitation skills
and gave me a meaning, a framework and style. I learned new talents
that helped me become more creative, yet simple and easy. One of
the major things I learned is graphic facilitation; it makes the inclusion and participation of all participants very easy, practical and
spontaneous. The spirit that reigns at the Coady makes one act with
inspiration and confidence. Being surrounded by like-minded people
boosts my creativity, confidence, productivity, and above all, it makes
me happy, supported and at ease. I was privileged to work with
Coady staff in Antigonish and in Egypt and took part in forming the
Coady Graduates Network in Egypt. The Coady spirit keeps me on
the learning side wherever I am and I am grateful for this.

nanci lee, Canada

I am a Chinese-Syrian poet and adult educator working at
Tatamagouche Centre, Nova Scotia. Grants (now gone), loans and
community bursaries made it possible for me to study so I care
a lot about equity and community's role in it. In 2002, I came
to Mi'kma'ki (Nova Scotia) to work on community or member-
owned finance and transformative adult education at the Coady.
My work has focused on economic models, small enough to focus

on relationships and shared ownership, networked enough to take on structural issues such as asset and inheritance rights and gender-based violence. I also believe deeply in sharing our stories, dialogue and meaning-making. For me, these are key to connecting, changing norms and narratives and collective healing.

Susan MacKay, Canada

I have over 20 years of experience working in various academic, educational, unionized and community environments. Enthusiastic about educational leadership, teaching and lifelong learning, my facilitation experience ranges from teaching English in Fukushima City, Japan; developing employment workshops for two career resource centres; facilitating international and specialty cuisine community cooking classes; leading groups through Laughter Yoga exercises; delivering anti-bullying education for a provincial union; and facilitating my own program, The PATH (Positive, Appreciative, Teamwork, Holistic) to Workplace Wellness. I am passionate about community development and working with anti-poverty organizations, in particular focused on food insecurity, energy poverty and affordable housing. Of all my professional experiences, my role as the Events and Public Education Co-ordinator at the Coady International Institute was one of the most impactful in my life. As an international event planner, it was a privilege to create Cooking with Coady, community cooking classes hosted by Coady participants, and organize numerous events in celebration of the 50th anniversary, including the India/Nepal Study Tour. Were it not for the experience of working at the Coady, which nourished my genuine interest in and deep concern for creating a more just and equitable world, I would not have applied for the Master of Adult Education program. With a heart full of gratitude, I thank the Program Teaching Staff whose encouragement and mentorship was foundational to me becoming an adult educator.

Suran Maharjan, Nepal

I am a development practitioner by profession and by passion. I was inspired to be in this sector from my childhood as I was active in a child club in my hometown. I grew up as an engaged and active citizen for community development and learned various approaches to development. Following the same passion, I volunteered in several organizations and campaigns after school and focused my post-secondary studies in the area of social science and development. I hold a master's degree in Co-operation and Development from the Institute for Advanced Studies, University of Pavia (Italy), with a specialization in development economics and project management. I am a 2009 Diploma graduate of the Coady International Institute and served as an Education Program Assistant in 2012. Currently, I am working as the Youth Program Manager in VSO Nepal where my focus is strengthening the outcomes of youth contributions. Prior to VSO, I was with Action Aid International Nepal where I developed and facilitated the Global Citizen training course for youth from Denmark and Nepal. In my early career, in 2008 I co-founded Xplore International that worked on the theme Information and Communications for Development (ICT4D). I have a special aptitude for using technologies for development.

Victoria Morcos, Egypt

I am grateful for the opportunity to share the tremendous self-discovery and turning point experiences I had during my time at the Coady International Institute in 2014 when I accomplished the *Diploma in Development Leadership*. The adult education methodologies had a great impact on my life and career path, especially considering I had been a management professional for 16 years working in the multinational corporate sector. I also have seven years in the development sector on USAIDS projects and at AUEED (Association of Upper Egypt for Education & Development) on development resources. During those years, my implicit, yet hidden passion for development appeared in my engagement in different charity activities. Upon returning to Egypt, I became an active member in the Coady Graduates Network (CGN); a co-founder of Haddouta Mesreya Development Association; and, co-facilitator with other CGN friends transferring our learnings to NGOs. Currently I am working as a freelance development consultant, applying the adult education approach. My Diploma in Translation French/Arabic, France (2004), BSc in Languages, Egypt (1988) and mixed work experience, equipped me with practical skills in development that were crystallized at the Coady. My passion for adult education became my lifestyle and part of my own development of practical human values in communications as well as an approach to awaken people through counselling, especially traumatized women in my community. My dream is to contribute to planting the seeds of love and understanding in human beings to make the world a better place to live.

Alice Ndlovu, Zimbabwe

I am a development practitioner with 12 years of experience working with grassroots organizations and communities in livelihoods, gender, child protection and agriculture programs. I hold a master's degree in Development Studies from Midlands State University; a *Certificate in Working with Children at Risk* from University of Kwazulu Natal, South Africa; a *Certificate in Building on Local and Indigenous Knowledges for Community Resilience*; *Community Driven Health Impact Assessment*; and, a *Diploma in Development Leadership* from the Coady International Institute. Currently, I work as the Administration and Operations Director for Muonde Trust through locally-driven educational, agricultural and community extension programs, and a healthy dose of action research, backing indigenous development efforts that maintain the connections between spirit, community and ecology. I have a wealth of experience in livelihoods, research and working with Indigenous communities in dealing with issues of climate change and different innovations. Before joining Muonde, I worked as a Livelihood Officer with the Bethany Project implementing livelihood programs with a variety of local people. I have also co-facilitated two regional workshops in Kenya and Ghana on *Building on Local and Indigenous Knowledges for Community Resilience*. These workshops enabled me to interact and visit different Indigenous communities. I have co-authored an article entitled, "Climate Change and Social Sustainability: A case of polycentric sustainabilities." I have a passion for Indigenous knowledge systems, gender and climate change.

Daren Okafo, Canada

For the past 25 years, I've tried to make sense of how community, creativity, technology and learning combine to enable spaces for collective recognition, identification and response to injustice, inequity and oppression. In 2001, while working at CKDU

Radio in Halifax, I took up a youth fellowship position at the Coady International Institute, ostensibly exploring innovative approaches to education and public information — that's early 2000's lingo for the web-tech guy! The open curiosity, the warmth of staff and the passion for shared, critical adult learning and grounded community innovation was overwhelming and my brief internship provided the fertile ground for launching what has become an integrated career in adult learning, learning innovations and technology, both at the Coady and beyond. More recently, I've been the head of Innovations and Research at the Irish National Adult Literacy Agency and managed learning programs at the Community Sector Council of Nova Scotia. My broader identity as a new media technologist and artist plays a significant role in my work as an adult educator and learning technologist, and I've endeavoured to carefully integrate these often divergent elements into an integrated practice. Before leaving Antigonish, I synthesized my experience as a technologist, educator and learner into a Master of Adult Education degree, bringing full circle my experience of learning, guidance and mentorship under the gifted and heart-centric team of educators, thinkers and change-makers at the Coady that I've come to call friends and family.

Mary Ramsis, Egypt

I am a facilitator and community development practitioner with more than 20 years of diversified experience. I work with different community groups and grassroots organizations supporting them to discover their own power to lead change in their lives through partnership strengthening and knowledge sharing. I am a 2011 graduate of the Coady International Institute's *Diploma in Development Leadership* who experienced personal transformation through the program. I was influenced by the Coady's worldview of using adult education strategies for leadership and empowerment. I went on to do further research for a master's degree in Participation, Power and Social Change at the Institute of Development Studies, University of Sussex. This study, in addition to the Coady's reflective experience, inspired me to empower community groups using action research methodology to develop and appreciate their local knowledge. This is what I am applying in my current capacity as a Program Manager at Drosos Foundation, relying on the values and the essence of adult education as core principles of community empowerment. I am always learning, whether formally or informally, following my interests in leadership, learning organizations, adult learning and power analysis. I am a co-founder, active member and animator with the Egypt Coady Graduates Network. I also co-coordinated a partnership project involving Coady grads in Egypt focusing on transparency and accountability in governance; and, as a research fellow helping pilot the Coady Connects platform for graduates. My experience at the Coady helps me to live and spread development values that put human beings at the heart of all the professional or volunteer work I do.

CS Reddy, India

I have over 30 years of experience in the development sector, particularly in the microfinance and livelihood sectors focusing on community-based models of microfinance and livelihoods. I am founder and CEO of APMAS and President of Sadhikaratha Foundation, two Indian not-for-profit national level technical support organizations with a vision of a sustainable women's self-help movement in India. For eight years I taught international certificate courses on community-based microfinance in Canada, Ethiopia and India with the Coady International Institute. I work closely with Government of India and State Governments of Andhra Pradesh, Bihar, Odisha, Telangana, West Bengal and Uttar Pradesh on various policy issues and provide advice on program implementation. I have written and spoken about the women's Self-Help Group (SHG) movement in India and am passionate about creating strategies to sustain it. I provide leadership in promoting self-regulation of SHGs and their federations, promoting farmer producer organizations (FPOs) as viable business entities engaged in agriculture value-chains and facilitating Government-NGO collaboration to maximize impact. I have the pleasure of leading a national network of major SHG promoters called ENABLE to engage in evidence-based policy advocacy.

Maina Wambugu Sebastian, Kenya

I have more than 28 years of rich experience in community-driven interventions and integrated initiatives acquired while working for several profit and public benefit organizations. I am currently working for Youth Action for Rural Development (YARD), an organization

I founded and which has grown to become a regional powerhouse touching the lives of thousands of people, especially farmers, children and women. Along with YARD, I have held many Board positions with other NGOs, schools, CBOs and faith-based institutions. Over time, I have acquired many competencies that have enabled me to participate and add value at policy and implementation levels. My uniqueness derives from the fact I have had to overcome many challenges, which have also acted as my motivators, to reach my current level. I grew up with multiple challenges including working as a small child to pay my school fees. In 2019, the Ministry of Agriculture and Co-operative Development appointed me as one of the Directors of the New Kenya Planters Co-operative Union-NKPCU, a new state corporation with a total of 750,000 smallholder coffee farmers and 3,000 coffee estate growers across the country. Our mandate is to help bring coffee back into profitability and earn incomes for the farmers through good farm practices, milling, marketing and value addition.

maureen st. clair, Grenada

I am a community and relationship builder, artist, peace educator, activist and writer. Born and raised in Canada, and with Grenadian citizenship, I have lived in Grenada, West Indies for more than 25 years. The Grenada Revolution was an impetus towards finding my own path rooted in transformative popular education. I have worked on a multitude of development projects with various Grenadian NGOs and community-based organizations over the years and am one of the co-founders of the Grenada Listening Project. For over 15 years I was an Associate of the Coady International Institute facilitating courses such as Foundations in Leadership, Adult Education and Community Development, and Community Conflict Transformation and Peacebuilding. My passion lies in creating brave, inclusive spaces that enable people collectively to do the work of self- and community-healing and building with a social justice and trauma-informed lens. I am deeply committed to the power of compassionate communication and the creative arts as pathways to personal and social transformation.

Dániel Törő, Hungary

I am a knowledge management consultant at the Food and
Agriculture Organization (FAO) with a background in international development and social studies. My main interest is connecting
people around their common interests to learn from each other
in order to change. My work focuses on designing and facilitating
virtual learning network events and managing thematic exchanges
among policy practitioners. By providing support to management
of an FAO-EU partnership program, which is implemented in 20
countries around the world, I am gaining new experiences and learning every day about how networks function and behave. Previously I
worked as a project co-ordinator for EduCare in Dharamsala, India,
involved in establishing community based youth networks and self-
help groups. My experience includes working on the implementation
of the internal knowledge management and communication strategy
for UNICEF's Supply Division in Copenhagen, Denmark. I have also
worked as an intern for the Hungarian Delegation to the European
Parliament.

Lazarus Udayakumar, India

I entered the field of development by chance, not by choice, as I
had wanted to become a teacher. I had been dreaming of one day
going to the Coady International Institute to attend the *Diploma in
Development Leadership*. It had been a dream for 28 years! When it
became a reality in 2014, my view of community development and
leadership was transformed. I am thankful for the transformation the
experience brought in my career. Certificates such as *Building Resilient
Communities* and *Learning Organization and Change* had a great
impact on me and I try to effectively apply what I learned in my on-go-
ing work with communities and organizations. Since 1981, I have been
involved in working for the development of disadvantaged people from
all walks of life from the grassroots to policy-making levels. I worked
with two organizations based in Germany and then with a grassroots
level community organization in India. I am now a freelance consultant offering services to NGOs in projects, road mapping, networking
and leadership. My special focus is working with Coady graduates in
India and helping them with their projects. Currently I am involved in
a transformative project with two other Coady graduates.

Corey Wesley, Anishinabek Nation

I am an award-winning social entrepreneur and an active member in my community of Thunder Bay, Ontario, Canada. I specialize in working with youth and Indigenous populations as a Sport & Occupational Performance Coach, as well as a traveling motivational speaker. I am a member of the Nishnawbe-Aski Nation, which consists of 49 First Nation Indigenous communities of Cree and Ojibway heritage in Northern Ontario. As a Master of Kinesiology graduate with a minor in Economics, I attended the *Learning Organizations and Change Certificate* at the Coady International Institute in 2017 to further my strengths in contributing to the betterment of Indigenous communities in my home territory. I am also a husband and father of four children, who are highly active in music, ice hockey and gymnastics.

Acknowledgements

This book took shape on the ancestral and unceded territory of the Mi'kmaw Nation. It would never have materialized without the dedication and enthusiasm of the 26 authors who shared their stories and helped us to see the sprouting of transformative change in themselves and their communities. The hard work was writing the stories during a global pandemic, in the midst of busy and active lives, often on the front lines trying to respond to the crisis. More importantly, we thank them for doing the work — over years, decades and lifetimes — to bring the values and principles they believe in to construct an equitable and just world into being. They have nurtured the seeds of learning and helped them to grow.

Our thanks also goes to Denise Davies, David MacDonald and Sue Adams — volunteer partners extraordinaire! Denise helped in the early days of conceptualizing the book and planning a strategy for marketing and dissemination. David offered his talent and skills to create the design and layout of the book you see. Sue applied her keen eye to ensure consistency in the overall style of the essays and helped us to polish them for our readers.

We appreciate the artistic contributions of nanci lee for the poems appearing on pages 58 and 100, and Darren C Brown for the illustrations that appear on the section title pages. Creativity is at the heart of transformation.

We also want to thank Dr. Maureen Coady who graciously contributed the foreword, and to Dr. Emily Sikazwe, Saloni Singh, Wayn Hamilton and Dr. Rajesh Tandon who read the manuscript and provided a comment in advance to encourage others to read the book.

As an editorial team this second book project helped make the unusual times of the pandemic meaningful as we worked together and with the larger group of authors to bring these powerful voices and experiences to light.

Finally, our thanks goes to all those who have been companions through the years in planting seeds of radical education, sometimes in challenging circumstances, and maintaining their commitment to seeing those seeds sprout, grow and thereby change communities around the world.

Be peace.
David, Debbie and Olga